I0022841

Ship Repair Technical Superintendent's Guide

Engr. Mohammed Khamis Mohammed

Professional Ship Repair Project Manager & Independent Marine Surveyor Consultancy.

FOREWORD

I feel honored to write a "foreword" for a book which is based on the engineering profession specifically from the "Shipping Industry". This industry is my core profession and primary experience which I've enjoyed for a span of 40 long years.

This is the second book by the author based on "transfer of knowledge" for professionals and peers of the shipping industry.

The best part by which I am impressed by this "masterpiece" of engineering is that it's not only for the professionals but also assists and helps the "novice" in shipping.

I recall one good November 2009 morning in a shipyard where my vessel had docked for emergency repairs. I was introduced to a young and handsome engineer as the in-charge person from the shipyard for my ship.

On my first meeting, I was impressed by the knowledge of the in-charge person and his work already done on my ship – this was author Eng. Mohammed Khamis!

The "Technical Superintendent Guide" covers topics which were never shared by any professional and may be considered trade secrets for any other practical reason.

The author has written and covered topics which give general and specific terms and knowledge to general managers, technical superintendents, DPA's and all "on shore" teams before a ship enters dry dock. The details given are not only knowledge but are instructions and guidelines for navigation/engineer officers, including the crew, to ascertain the readiness in cutting "downtime" in shipyards.

Conclusions: I remind the readers that both books by the author "Ship Repairs Project Management" and this second edition "The Technical Superintendent Guide" are very unique firsthand knowledge translated into a "book" and is a must read to be circulated among colleagues.

I wish Godspeed and continuous success to the author.

Fuad Hashmi
Director technical
Sis ship charterer LLC Dubai
Dated: Jan. 02, 2019.

Introduction

As I have mentioned in the earlier introduction of my first book "Ship Repair Project Managers Guide" that the ship repair activities are considered the heart and focus of interest at any shipyard.

In this book I can say that the ship operation activity is considered the heart and focus of interest for any ship owner companies. The main purpose of this guide is to make it available to all ship managements and their ship technical superintendents as a ready reference. The role of ship repair management should be considered by ship technical superintendents as very important in staying aware that he is the owner's representative to the shipyard in the project he is handling.

To assist all new technical superintendents in performing the repair activities, I have written this guidebook based on my own practical work experiences. It is my hope that ship technical superintendents everywhere will benefit from this guide.

Engr. Mohammed Khamis Mohammed
Bachelor's Degree of Marine and Naval Architecture Engineering, Alexandria University, Faculty of Engineering, Egypt.

Experience: Professional Ship Repair Project Manager | Independent Marine Surveyor Consultancy.

Table of Contents

FREE Bonuses

Thank you very much for purchasing this book. First of all, before you read ahead, please **register your book** here and get the FREE bonuses of this book:

https://books10.org/superintendent-book

As a Ship Repair Superintendent's Guide **Book Club member**, you will receive lots of benefits and support from our Book Club.

Certification Program

This is the official book for taking the **ProjectManagers.Org Certified Ship Repair Project Manager (SRPM)** program:

https://projectmanagers.org/superintendent-certification

This Career Program will improve your job opportunities and certify your skills gained from this book.

The Certification Exam is online, and once you sign up you can take it whenever you want (no deadline limits). Just sign up today for your exam and start enjoying this book.

Chapter 1: The General Terms and Definitions in the Ship Repair

1.1. Ship Repair Yard

The organization for or in relation to ship repair, conversion, maintenance & reconstruction using yard facilities, personnel and equipment as an entity performing the work inside the dry dock, on berth, at anchorage area.

1.2. Ship Repair Yard Customer/ Ship Owner

Any person, ship owner, ship management or ship operator who has agreed to the work with the yard in accordance with a contract.

1.3. Technical Superintendent/Owner Representative

A party or parties duly authorized and nominated by the ship owner to act on behalf of the owners with whom the class surveyors, service engineers and ship repair yard may consult at all reasonable times and whose instructions, requests, and decisions are issued.

1.4. Vessel

Any ship, barge, rig or other marine craft which is to be subject of work.

1.5. Customer Staff/Ship Crew

The party or parties responsible for the operation of customer equipment.

1.6. Ship Repair Tender

A quotation covering price, time, and terms to carry out work as described in the customer's specification.

1.7. The Repair Work

All tasks to be performed by the ship repair yard, ship crew, services engineers or subcontractors in accordance with the repair specifications, including all changes of scope as agreed with a customer representative/ technical superintendent.

1.8. The Ship Repair Project

Any contracted work between the yard and customer for performance of ship repair, conversion, docking, and related services.

1.9. The Repair Specification

A technical description of the repair work as described by ship technical superintendent in the customer's specification with reservation, exclusions, conditions, and remarks introduced by the tender and agreed according to the contract.

1.10. Ship Repair Yard Representative/Ship

Repair Manager

The party or parties nominated by the yard to liaise between customer representative and yard for leading, coordinating, and managing the performance of specific projects is generally identified as the ship repair manager.

1.11. Safety Rules

A set of safety rules and procedures based on international standards, local government rules, and common practices, binding to the ship owner and compulsory to the ship repair yard.

1.12. The Class Surveyor

A party or parties nominated by the classification society bureau, to verify whether the international maritime rules and regulations are applicable on-board the ship during the dry docking and sea going operation.

1.13. The Flag State Control Officers

A party or parties nominated by the flag administrations to verify whether the flagged vessels are complying with applicable international conventions on safety, pollution prevention, crew living and working conditions.

1.14. The Port State Control Officers

A party or parties nominated by the port administration to verify whether foreign flagged vessels are complying with applicable international conventions on safety, pollution prevention and crew living and working conditions. Where vessels are found to be not in substantial compliance, the PSC system imposes actions to ensure they are brought into compliance.

1.15. Overall survey

Is a survey intended to report on the overall condition of the hull structure and determine the extent of additional close-up surveys.

1.16. Close-up survey

Is a survey where the details of structural components are within the close visual inspection range of the surveyor, i.e. preferably within reach of hand.

1.17. Annual Survey

Is a survey to be carried out yearly with a three-month window, in either way from its due date, at each Annual Survey, the general condition of hull, machinery and equipment of the ship is examined by the surveyors at the ship's afloat condition.

1.18. Intermediate Survey

Is a survey to be carried out at two-and-half year intervals with a six-month window in either way from its due date between special surveys At each Intermediate Survey, the condition of hull, machinery and equipment of the ship are examined by the surveyors to an intermediate extent between Special Survey and Annual Survey.

1.19. Special Survey

Is a survey to be carried at four-year intervals; One year of grace may be given. At each Special Survey, the condition of hull, machinery and equipment are thoroughly examined by the surveyors normally by placing the ship in dry dock. The extent of examination becomes more thorough for aged ship, the severest examinations being required for ships of over fifteen years of age.

1.20. Ship Certificates

A certificate, required under existing law, issued for a ship, or a part of a ship, with reference to codes or conventions issued by IMO or ILO or to national legislation.

Chapter 2: Familiarization with Ship Company Organization Roles

It is very important to you as technical superintendent to know the internal responsibilities of each person in your company organization that is related to ship operation.

Here I will give you a brief idea about the organization of the ship Owner Company, BUT this is not a standard organization because it can be different form one Owner Company to another.

1.21. General Manager (GM)

The General Manager has the following responsibilities:

- Ensures that Company Management System is overall implemented
- Insurance claims
- Promotes the need for safety operations, as well as the responsibilities of all employees towards the protection of the environment and protection of all assets under his care
- Ensures that the Company consistently and continuously meets its contractual obligations

- Ensures that sufficient staff of necessary experience and qualification, are recruited, retained and trained where necessary in order to maintain the required operational standards
- Total responsibility of the Company towards safe operation and pollution prevention awareness on all the ships under the control of the Company

1.22. Accounting Department

- Responsible to the General Manager for all the accounts of the Company

- Monitors expenses in relation to budgets such as spare parts supply, fuel supply, lubrication oil supply, provision supply, painting supply, service providers fees and schedule the payments.

1.23. Technical Manager (TM)

- Responsible for the total technical management of all the ships including purchasing, preventive maintenance programs, safety and oil pollution prevention

- Responsible to the General Manager for all aspects of safety, pollution prevention protection and continuous improvement programs to keep abreast of changing technology and industry standards.

1.24. Designated Person Ashore (DPA)

The DPA has direct access to the General Manager on all matters concerning:

- Safety of human life, property, cargoes and ships

- Protection of environment from pollution

- Formulation and amendment of the policies of the Company as found necessary

- Proper implementation of these policies through the channels of the relevant departments

- Analysis and review of the feedback from the ships concerning these policies and recommend any required changes

- Planning of audits, training and selection of internal auditors

- Collection and evaluation of all records in conjunction with the relevant departments

- Ensures adequacy of resources, both in the Office and onboard all the ships to provide the necessary support for successful implementation of the policies

- The Company is responsible for ensuring that adequate resources and shore-based support are provided to enable the Designated Person to carry out his functions

1.25. Operations Manager (OM)

- Total responsibility for ship's chartering, Company policy disputes, and ship's Company policy performance

- Responsible for all ship management functions including manning agents, supervision of vessels and insurance claims

1.26. Port Captain

- Responsible to the Operational Manager for proper and sufficient manning of the ships with qualified personnel

- Co-ordination of travel

- Joining arrangements of shipboard staff through manning agents

- Strict implementation of Drug and alcohol policy of the Company

1.27. Superintendent Engineer

- Responsible to the Technical Manager for safe, efficient and clean operation of ships

- Directly in contact with ships to provide support for repair, supplies, maintenance for efficient operation

- Ensures implementation of Company policies, invites the scrutinizing

- Constructive criticism from the ships for continuous improvement in policy matters

- Coordinates inspections of classification societies, flag state, insurance and schedule personal inspection of ships for proper control

- Formulate budget and monitor the expenses on regular basis

- Investigate and report accidents, near misses for preventing a reoccurrence and sharing this experience with other ships in the fleet

1.28. Company Security Officer

- Means the person designated by the company for ensuring that the ship security assessment is carried out, that a ship security plan is developed and submitted for approval and implemented. Thereafter, it is maintained for liaison with the port facility security officers and the ship security officer.

- To provide a link with the ship security officer (SSO) & port facilities security officer (PFSO)

- To ensure that all the appropriate actions have been taken accordance with the ship security plan (SSP)

- Co-ordinate ship's action to implement measures and instructions given by the authorities

Chapter 3: Familiarization with the Engine Room Instructions

The technical superintendent is responsible for ship operation in safe and good condition according to company policies with applicable international conventions on safety, pollution prevention and crew living and working conditions.

In order to reach the above mentioned, the technical superintendent should be familiar with the ship operation instructions for engine room and bridge/ deck crew.

In this chapter I will give you a brief idea about the engine room crew duties on-board the ship.

For the bridge/deck crew instructions, it will be described in chapter 4.

3.1. Engine Room Crew Duties

The C/E shall keep the ship Master advised of all matters relating to E/R staff, technical maintenance of the vessel and the operational state of equipment under his control.

The C/E and the Master are to come to a clear understanding on the procedures to be adopted and followed for engine maneuvers in circumstances of reduced visibility, upon entering confined/pilot age waters, and in the event of sudden emergencies. The following procedures are to be clearly stated in writing and posted on the Bridge and in the Engine Control Room:

- Main Engine Failure
- Black Out
- Collision or Stranding
- Steering Gear Failure

3.1.1. Chief Engineer

The Chief Engineer Officer is responsible to the ship Master and the Company technical superintendent for the following:

a) The technical maintenance of the vessel and all its equipment.

b) The safe operation of all machinery and equipment on board.

c) The administration of the Technical Department.

d) The supervision of all repairs carried out by shore contractors.

3.1.2. Second Engineer/1st Assistant Engineer

The Second Engineer/1st Assistant Officer is responsible to the C/E for the efficient running and maintenance of all technical equipment except Radio and Navigational Aids. In the absence of the C/E, the 2nd Engineer will deputise for him on all matters.

3.1.3. Communications with the Company

The C/E is to keep the Master advised on all occasions when he wishes to communicate directly with the Company Technical Superintendent.

3.1.4. Discipline

The C/E is responsible for the supervision and discipline of all members of his staff and for ensuring that they observe all Company Standing Instructions.

3.1.5. Reports - Officers and Ratings

The C/E is responsible for completing the staff appraisal form for those personnel in his department and forwarding it to the Company.

3.1.6. Repairs

The ship Master's agreement must be obtained before undertaking any repair work which necessitates immobilising the vessel's engines or reducing the standby power (electrical) capacity.

3.1.7. Speed and Fuel Consumption

Strict economy in consumption of bunkers is to be observed where reasonably practicable.

The Master, in consultation with the C/E, will decide upon the vessel's service speed between ports in order to maintain the schedules required by the Owner/ Charterer.

3.1.8. Freshwater

The C/E is to confer with the Chief Officer concerning the quantity of fresh water to be carried and is to exercise strict control over the use of fresh water in the engine room.

The Chief Officer and C/E must closely liaise on the daily consumption of fresh water.

The soundings of freshwater tanks must be entered daily in the Deck Log Book.

3.1.9. Joining and Leaving

The off-signing C/E must prepare The Handover Report and discuss them with the on-signing C/E.

All C/E's are required to complete this form and send a copy to the Company.

3.1.10. Inspections

The C/E is to be at all times familiar with the condition of the vessel and/or equipment under his control.

He is to accompany the Master on inspections of the vessel and is to co-operate fully with other Departments to preserve the efficiency of the vessel.

3.1.11. Engine Room Logbooks

The Engine Room Logbook is to be completed in ink by the Duty Engineer.

The C/E is to enter all the additional information required by these instructions and sign the Logbook daily.

On occasions where the main engine is not running at these times the C/E is to ensure that, where reasonably practicable, all engine pressures and temperatures are recorded along with the status of all plant (e.g. parts dismantled for repair or inspection etc.).

The Logbook is to be kept clean and it is essential that only factual information is recorded.

The original of the Engineers Logbook is to be forwarded to the office when completed.

3.1.12 Fire and Safety Regulations

The C/E must endeavour to ensure that all members of his staff are made aware of all Company, statutory, local authority and installation fire and safety regulations, and that such legislations are strictly adhered to.

He is to ensure that all safety equipment assigned to those parts of the vessel under his direct control are properly maintained and, in particular,

He is also to satisfy himself that lifeboat engines and emergency electrical and mechanical equipment are at all times ready for use.

The C/E is also to be actively involved in the vessel's Safety Committee meetings.

He is to liaise with the designated officer with regard to checking and maintaining fire protection equipment throughout the vessel.

3.1.13. Allocation of Watch Keeping Duties

The C/E is to allocate watch-keeping duties to his staff, ensuring that a competent Officer is always in charge of the machinery spaces.

When the vessel is in port, the C/E is to ensure that either himself or the 2nd Engineer/1st Assistant is available at any time.

When the vessel is navigating in pilot age waters, during river transits and at all times as directed by the Master, the Chief Engineer must ensure that sufficient qualified personnel are on duty in the engine room.

Under no circumstances whatsoever is the engine room rating, or any other personnel, authorised to answer any alarm condition in the engine room.

3.1.14. Accident Prevention

The C/E is to make every effort to promote Accident Prevention on board the vessel.

He is to ensure that his staff is fully conversant with the correct operating methods for all machinery.

Particular attention is to be paid to instructing staff in correct procedure for lighting boiler oil fuel burners and opening up any pressure vessel for internal inspection.

A routine should be established for checking and recording the condition of all hand tools and portable equipment, particular attention should be given to any electrical connections and cables.

3.1.15. Duty Engineer - Responsibilities

The Duty Engineer is directly responsible to the C/E and has full authority over the safe and economic operation of the main and auxiliary machinery during his duty period.

Before being relieved, the Duty Engineer will complete all entries, as required, in the Engineers Logbook. The relief Duty Engineer will carry out a thorough examination of machinery spaces before taking over responsibility for the next duty period.

He ensures that the main engines are running or manoeuvring in accordance with requirements, providing the electrical power necessary for navigational and operational equipment, including steering gear.

3.2. CARE OF MACHINERY AND VESSEL

The main and auxiliary machinery includes different engines from various manufacturers. Instruction manuals dealing with the correct operation of machinery and equipment etc. are supplied to each vessel. These manuals, together with the Planned Maintenance Systems, must be used for the satisfactory operation and maintenance of machinery and equipment.

In addition, the Company maintains each vessel in compliance with Charterers' and Owners' written and recorded requirements.

To supplement this, specific items of machinery are maintained on a running hour's schedule, based on manufacturer's recommendations and operational experience.

The Chief Engineer keeps maintenance records and copies are sent to the TM on a monthly basis.

3.2.1. Alarms

All machinery protection devices and alarms must be tested at a maximum of 3-month intervals.

Should any protection device or alarm become defective, the C/E must be advised immediately in order that he can decide upon the necessary precautions to be taken until the equipment has been repaired.

3.2.2. Operation of Machinery in an Emergency

In all vessels, the manufacturer's instructions regarding the operation of the main machinery under normal service conditions must be strictly adhered to except under emergency conditions involving the saving of life or the safety of the vessel.

In such cases, entries are to be made in the relevant logbook(s).

3.2.3. Planned Maintenance Systems

The Planned Maintenance Systems are designed to incorporate as many items as possible of the vessel's equipment.

It is important that maintenance work adheres to the schedule and that the required records are properly maintained.

The frequencies given for overhauls/inspections are, and can only be, guidelines.

The trading pattern of the vessel, climatic conditions and operational circumstances must be carefully considered and, when necessary, frequencies increased to cater to the prevailing conditions.

The frequencies quoted should therefore be looked upon as minimum.

3.2.4. Critical Equipment and Systems

The Company have identified the following equipment and systems as being critical in that should they fail, may result in a hazardous situation

Systems identified for programmed testing within the planned maintenance system are:

Hull & Cargo Systems

Watertight closures
Vents
Cargo Gear
Bilge System and Equipment

Safety

Fire lines, Pumps, Hydrants and Hoses
CO_2 System
Fixed Gas Extinguishing System
Breathing Apparatus and Fireman's Outfits

Fire Detection and Alarm System
Internal Communications
Fire Dampers, Vents and Stops
Lifeboats, Davits and Equipment
Life rafts, Release System, and Equipment
Lifejackets, Lifebuoys, and Flotation Aids
Instruction Notices and Plans
EPIRBS and Transponders
Permit to Work Systems and Personal Safety Equipment

Bridge

Radars
Navigation Lights and Shapes
Ships, Gong and Whistle
Gyro and Repeaters
Auto Pilot and Steering Stand
Rudder Indicators
Signal Lamp
ME Control System and Emergency Stop
Internal Communications Equipment
Echo Sounder
Magnetic Compass
Charts and Publications
Standby/Backup Equipment and Systems

Radio

Main Radio
Emergency Radio

Emergency Batteries
EPIRBS & SARTS

Each failure of this equipment or systems is a non-conformance.

3.2.5. Specialised Equipment

Specialised items of equipment may require maintenance by shore-based technicians.

In these circumstances the vessel advises the Company's TM or his technical superintendent makes the necessary arrangements for a suitable technician to attend.

3.2.6 Deck Maintenance

General deck maintenance is on-going under the supervision of the OM and the day-to-day supervision of the Master.

A record of work carried out is forwarded to the office by the Master (and Chief Engineer where appropriate).

All maintenance and repairs are recorded in the vessels filing system and copies forwarded to the Company.

Vessel defects are notified to the OM or the technical superintendent by Defect Reports or may be telexed if the operational capacity of the vessel is affected.

These reports are used to assist in the formulation of a running repair list, which forms the basis for riding squad repairs and docking repair lists.

3.2.7. Engine Maintenance

Engine and machinery maintenance are an on-going operation under the supervision of the S/E and the day-to-day supervision of the Chief Engineer. Records of maintenance are forwarded on a monthly basis to the TM or the technical superintendent.

All maintenance and repairs are recorded in the Vessel's Filing System (VFS) and copies are forwarded to the Company.

3.2.8. Electrical Maintenance

Electrical, navigational and communications equipment are maintained under the day-to-day supervision of the Master and Chief Engineer.

Status reports are forwarded periodically which include operational efficiency of equipment and insulation test results.

All records of maintenance and repairs are maintained in the ship file.

3.2.9. Reliability of Equipment

In order to maintain an efficient record of reliability of equipment, it is required that reports shall be made on any operating problems experienced.

3.2.10. Main Engine Trials

Engines must not be turned or trials carried out until the Duty Engineer has confirmed with the Master that the propeller is clear, moorings are adequate, and it is safe to do so.

When preparing the main engine for manoeuvring after completion of repairs, or after a period in port or at anchor, a full turn shall be made observing the open indicator cocks, after which the turning gear will be disengaged, thus ensuring that all moving parts are free and clear of fuel and water prior to further testing.

Before starting the main engine, it must be turned on air, with the cylinder indicator cocks open.

3.2.11. Lubricating Oils

Irrespective of the vessel's trading pattern, the Company requires the taking of lubricating oil samples on a regular basis, as directed by the supplier.

The intervals for the taking of these samples must not exceed the following:

Main Engine: (slow speed)   -4 months
Stern Tube   -   6 months
Alternators   -   4 months
Other auxiliaries, hydraulic systems etc. 4 months

The samples taken from the main engine and the auxiliary engines must be a representative sample with the oil in circulation.
It is important that all samples are subsequently taken from the same location.

The instructions supplied with the sample kit are to be strictly adhered to when the samples are drawn and sent for analysis.

The Laboratory will send the analysis results to the Company.

The Chief Engineer will immediately be informed of any abnormalities.

The stern tube system must be tested monthly for water using the on-board test kit and the results recorded in the E/R logbook.

When receiving large quantities of lubricating oil, a sample must be drawn and retained on board until the next delivery of lubricating oil has been received on board.

The main engine sump must be fully charged as recommended by the manufacturer.

The main engine lubricating oil must be continuously centrifuged and, when circumstances permit, the engine charge will be transferred to the renovating tank for heating, settling and subsequent return to the crank case through the centrifuge.

All lubricating oils must be ordered through the Company.

Should any contamination be suspected, the oil samples should be landed at the first available port and the necessary steps taken to prevent machinery damage.

The lubricating oil purifiers must be continuously monitored and maintained to provide optimum efficiency.

The C/E must be vigilant to ensure that the lubrication systems are not contaminated by water.

Masters and Chief Engineers must be aware that machinery damages resulting from the ingress of water into lubricating systems may not always be covered by underwriters, especially if it can be proved that the vessel's personnel have been negligent.

3.2.12. Electrical Installation

The number of alternators on load, either at sea or in port depends upon the vessel's operational and domestic requirements and must at all times be adequate to ensure the safe continuity of supply.

Under normal circumstances at sea only one alternator should be required.

During idle periods, main and emergency diesel alternators

are to be tested weekly and, where fitted, remote and automatic controls checked.

When the vessel is navigating in narrow waters, entering and leaving port, etc., the stand-by alternator must be in use and sharing the load on the main switchboard.

The vessel's shaft alternators, if fitted, must not be used for E/R or domestic loads when the vessel is navigating in pilot age waters or during river transits.

3.2.13. Auxiliary Machinery

In all cases where duplicate units are fitted, the operating time is to be equally shared between the two units.

All automatic changeover devices are to be tested when putting units into service and when shutting them down.

Shutdowns should be tested at regular intervals.

3.2.14. Boilers

Adjustment of safety valves - It is required that after every survey, the safety valves are to be adjusted to the correct safe working pressure.

This adjustment must be done to the satisfaction of the surveyor on the first occasion when steam is raised on the boiler.

Where the firing arrangements are such that normal working pressure of the boiler cannot be attained until the vessel is under way, the safety valves are to be adjusted by the Chief Engineer to the correct safe working pressure.

This is to be recorded in the vessel's logbook and the Classification Society and Company informed by telex or e-mail.

The logbook entry must be presented to the next attending Class Surveyor for verification and to complete the society's records.

The Company issues the following advice:

a) When the boilers are in service:

i)   Proper feed treatment should be administered at all times and alkalinity, suspended solids, and reserve levels maintained within the required parameters.

ii)   The boiler water tests are to be made at least twice weekly and recorded.

iii)   Maker's instructions should be followed.

b) During maintenance, routine cleaning and out of service periods:

i)   Boilers, when not in use, should either be kept full of water, which is alkaline or completely empty and dry and should be maintained in accordance with the manufacturer's instructions.

3.2.15. Emergency Steering Gear

The emergency steering gear is to be tested and the vessel steered from the emergency position for at least one hour every three months.

A suitable entry is to be made in the Engine Room Logbook recording the test, and the OLB (official log book) or deck log.

Instructions for the operation of emergency steering must be posted.

Further details on the SOLAS regulations for the testing of steering gear can be found in SOLAS Chapter V - Safety of Navigation.

These regulations shall be strictly adhered to and regarded as minimum requirements.

3.2.16. Continuous Survey of Machinery

Planned Maintenance is carried out by ship's staff and based on the CSM schedule.

Additionally, specific items of machinery have running hours recorded and maintenance schedules are based on manufacturer's recommendations, and operational experience.

It is the responsibility of the C/E to ensure that the CSM cycle is maintained up to date.

Where applicable the C/E will arrange to progress the CSM and forward to the Head Office a list of items completed.

Originals of Classification Interim Certificates are to be retained on board; duplicates are to be forwarded to the Company.

3.2.17. Stern Tubes

In vessels fitted with water cooled oil lubricated stern tubes, there must always be sufficient water in the lower after peak, (or stern tube cooling tank), to cover the stern tube before using the main engine.

3.2.18. Testing of Hold/Bilge Suction Lines

When testing hold bilge and suction lines there is a possibility for water to flood into the engine room,

To avoid this possibility the following practice should be adopted when carrying out these tests:

- Testing of the suctions is to be carried out using practical pumping tests.

- Leakage tests on the valves are to be carried out by pressurising the main. Conversely, an inspection as to the condition of the valves may be carried out in lieu of a pressure test, but verification as to the tightness of the valves must be ensured. Hold and ballast suction lines must not be subjected to a pressure greater than 3 bars during testing.

- Tests carried out should be entered in the Deck Logbook.

- All isolating and crossover valves between the ballast pumping systems and the hold/bilge suctions are to be shut and the pressure in the hold suction lines should be monitored to ensure that over-pressurising of the main is avoided.

- After pumping of ballast and bilges, the securing and isolating of these individual systems should be checked. The practice of just shutting the minimum number of valves to save time at future pumping must be avoided.

- During the voyage, soundings of holds should be taken daily.

- A record of the results should be kept in the Deck Logbook.

3.3. MONITORING

The effectiveness of the maintenance programs is monitored by:

- Classification Survey Reports and Periodical and Annual Listings

- The Company reporting system

- Planned maintenance system

- On board Inspections by Company's Management

- Charterers' and Owners' Inspections

- Internal Safety Audits

- Frequency of Machinery Failure and consequential off-hire periods.

3.4. STATUTORY/FLAG SURVEYS AND CLASSIFICATION

Surveys of hull, machinery, electrical and safety equipment are planned and carried out in accordance with the appropriate rules and regulations.

Certificates and periodical printouts from the vessel's Classification Society provide the necessary records of surveys and the next due date for survey.

Whenever a Planned Maintenance System is in place, it is co-ordinated with Class requirements in order to avoid duplication of overhauls or inspections.

The Chief Engineer in the vessels filing system maintains records.

If Class has approved the Planned Maintenance System, Continuous Machinery Surveys (excluding crankshafts, crankshaft bearings and pressure vessels) may be carried out by the Chief Engineer during planned maintenance overhauls, provided Class audits the Planned Maintenance System annually.

The Chief Engineer in the vessels filing system records such maintenance.

If the Chief Engineer has been given dispensation from Class to undertake Continuous Machinery Surveys, this is taken advantage of whether or not a formal Planned Maintenance System is in place and is recorded by the C/E in the vessels filing system maintained by the Technical Department.

Records of all surveys are kept in the appropriate files on board the vessel.

Copies of survey reports are also kept in the corresponding files in Technical Department for a minimum of 5 years.

Inspections by Port State Control and Flag State may be performed unannounced at any time. In such cases the Master, Chief Engineer and ship's staff must render full co-operation.

The above inspections take priority over commercial and operational considerations.

Summary reports are handed to the Master and retained in the VFS with copies to the Technical Department for the attention of the TM and OM.

Any non-conformity must be corrected immediately where this is not possible due to new equipment/spares being required,

The Technical Department are responsible for arranging the supply of such equipment.

The Technical Department will advise the inspecting authority when all non-conformities are corrected.

The vessel's statutory and trading certificates are retained on board for inspection by Port State Control/Flag/Class as appropriate.

3.5. DOCUMENTATION

Records and reports are kept on board in the Company's Vessel Filing System (VFS) at Deck and Engine Logbooks.

The Company in the VFS keeps copies of all records and reports from the vessel ashore.

In the event that a vessel leaves the Company's management, the VFS will be archived for a period in accordance with the Records Procedure or until any outstanding insurance claims are settled, whichever is the later and then destroyed.

3.6. SUB-CONTRACTORS

Where a vessel requires assistance from sub-contractors, a quote for the specified work is obtained whenever possible and approved by the TM or the technical superintendent before a purchase order is generated and the work authorised.

If the expenditure is not within the budget or is in excess of limits previously agreed with the top management, then the top management is advised.

It is the responsibility of the Master and/or Chief Engineer to monitor the performance of the work being carried out if a member of the shore management is not present.

On completion of the work, the Master and Chief Engineer are to sign for the work completed and verify that the hours on the time sheet are correct.

3.7. PREVENTION OF CRANKCASE EXPLOSIONS

Care must be taken to avoid the conditions that are necessary for a crankcase explosion to occur.

Excessive local normally causes these overheating of moving parts and/or blow past in the case of medium speed engines.

Checking of bearing clearances, crankcase inspections and regular LO analysis will significantly reduce the chances of a crankcase explosion occurring.

Where vessels are fitted with a mist detector, this unit is to be operational at all times.

In addition, routine inspection of the crankcase and feeling by hand for any hot spots should be carried out.

Where vessels are fitted with bearing temperature sensors, these should be closely monitored and any significant change in temperature investigated.

When a crankcase overheats, the engine should be slowed immediately and stopped as soon as possible.

The LO supply should be maintained, and the turning gear engaged and operated.

UNDER NO CIRCUMSTANCES MUST ANY CRANKCASE DOOR BE OPENED UNTIL THE ENGINE HAS COOLED DOWN.

THE ENGINE MUST NOT BE RESTARTED UNTIL THE CAUSE OF OVERHEATING HAS BEEN IDENTIFIED AND RECTIFIED.

3.8. OPERATIONAL INFORMATION

3.8.1. Valves - General

All valves that are not generally opened or closed frequently must be lubricated and regularly operated to ensure that they will operate in an emergency and recorded in the E/R logbook.

3.8.2. Stops - Scheduled and Unscheduled

Stops at sea, due to scheduled or unscheduled circumstances must be clearly defined in the Deck and Engine Room Logbooks.

Included in unscheduled stops will be any delays that interrupt cargo operations or cause delays during the period from End of Passage arrival to Full Away departure.

3.8.3. Emergencies

The following circumstances constitute an emergency requiring immediate action:

a) Fire or flooding in any space or compartment.

b) Difficulty in complying with orders received from the Bridge.

c) Difficulty in complying with instructions or standing orders for the proper operation of machinery.

In any one of the above circumstances, the Duty Engineer must immediately inform the officers on the Bridge and the C/E.

The Duty Engineer should not hesitate before taking immediate action to prevent an emergency situation deteriorating.

3.8.4. Alteration of Speed

Any alteration to the operational speed of the vessel must be agreed between the Master and the C/E.

If these conflicts with the instructions received from the Ship Company or Charterer, then the reasons for the alteration must be communicated to the Company, with full details recorded in the Deck and Engine Room Logbooks.

The Duty Engineer must not alter the vessel's speed (pitch or rpm, as applicable) without informing the officers on the Bridge beforehand, unless it is in response to orders direct from the Bridge or if exceptional circumstances in the engine room call for emergency action.

3.8.5. Starting Aids

All persons concerned with the operation of diesel engines are advised to bear in mind the dangers that can arise from the use of volatile low flash point starting fluids in engines, particularly those which are started by admission of compressed air to the cylinders.

Regardless of the engine starting arrangements, such fluids should always be used in accordance with the maker's instructions but never at the same time as cylinder or manifold heater plugs are being used or when the engine is hot.

3.8.6. Heavy Fuel Oil

Particular attention is drawn to the makers operation instructions for engines designed to operate constantly on heavy fuel oil.

The engine manufacturer's instructions must be observed with all engines when changing from heavy fuel oil to diesel oil operation.

Chapter 4: Familiarization with the Bridge/Deck Instructions

As I have mentioned in chapter 3 introduction that the technical superintendent is responsible for ship operation in safe and good conditions, and to reach this target, he should be familiar with the operation instructions to E/R and Bridge crew.

In this chapter I will give you a brief idea about the Bridge/Deck crew duties on-board the ship.

4.1. Bridge/Deck crew duties

4.1.1. CERTIFICATES

The Master is responsible for ensuring that all certificates are current and valid for his vessel and for the intended voyage.

The Company is responsible for monitoring the status and validity of the vessel's certificates.

The Company is to advise the Master of all surveys arranged.

4.1.2. Monitoring

Vessels are required to send to the Technical Manager (T.M.) or to the technical superintendent a list of the ship certificates once every three months.

Where new certificates have been issued or endorsements made to existing certificates, a copy of the relevant certificate should be attached to the list of certificates.

Where a statutory certificate is revalidated, a copy is to be forwarded to the technical superintendent.

Certificates for other surveys arranged by the Master are also to be copied to the company.

4.1.3. Arranging Surveys

The Master is responsible for advising the company of any due surveys and for arranging this locally if instructed so to do.

4.1.4. Equipment Certificate(s)

The Company is responsible for ensuring that all required certifiable spares and equipment supplied have a certificate valid for its strength or purpose.

The Master is responsible for ensuring that all locally purchased equipment has a certificate valid for its strength or purpose where required.

The Master is responsible for keeping in the equipment section of the vessel's filing system all equipment certificates.

Particular attention must be paid to certificates for ropes, wires and shackles.

Where ropes are supplied in coils the certificate must be marked as to the location where the rope is put into use.

4.2. INSPECTIONS

To ensure the vessels are operated effectively and efficiently, the Company operates a system of inspections carried out both by ships' staff with the technical superintendent.

4.2.1. Internal Audits

The DPA in conjunction with the Technical Manage (TM) and the technical superintendent will arrange for an Internal Safety Audit of each vessel annually in accordance with the Company's Internal Audit Schedule.

4.2.2. Unscheduled Inspections

The TM ensures that the Technical Superintendent Engineer directly responsible for the vessel visits at least twice per year and formulates full reports, which are evaluated by the TM.

The DPA may also visit the vessel to carryout inspections and conduct audits.

4.3. BILLS OF LADING

When a carrier takes goods into his charge, he must on demand issue to the shipper a bill of lading.

The Master of the vessel carrying the goods is accepted as acting on behalf of the carrier although a bill of lading may be signed by any person having authority from the carrier.

4.3.1. Contents

The bill of lading must include, amongst other things, the following particulars:

a) The general nature of the goods, the leading marks necessary for identification of the goods, an express statement, if applicable, as to the dangerous character of the goods, the number of package or pieces, and the weight of the goods or their quantity otherwise, expressed, all such particulars as furnished by the shipper.

b) The apparent condition of the goods.
c) The name and principal place of business of the carrier.

d) The name of the shipper.

e) The consignee if named by the shipper.

f)   The port of loading under the contract of carriage by sea and the date on which the goods were taken over by the carrier at the port of loading.

g) The port of discharge under the contract of carriage by sea.

h) The number of originals of the bill of lading, if more than one.

i)   The place of issuance of the bill of lading.

j)   The signature of the carrier or a person acting on his behalf.

k)   The freight to the extent payable by the consignee or other indication that freight is payable by him.

l)   The statement, if applicable, that the goods shall or may be carried on deck.

m) The date or the period of delivery of the goods at the port of discharge if expressly agreed upon between the parties.

4.3.2. Dangers

It is a common although dangerous practice to deliver a cargo to a receiver against the one original bill of lading carried on board as it is possible the party demanding delivery is not the rightful owner of the goods. Masters should always obtain a receipt if an original Bill of Lading is carried on board and handed over to a receiver.

It is possible that the party demanding delivery of the cargo has not acquired title to the cargo by reference to the original bills of lading and so a mis-delivery of the cargo may occur.

In order to minimise the risk when an original Bill of Lading is carried on-board, the following steps should be taken:

1) The Agent or Shipper should be instructed to add the following wording prominently to all three original bills of lading

"One original bill of lading retained on board against which bill delivery of cargo may properly be made on instructions received from shipper/charterer."

2) The person demanding delivery must correctly identify themselves.

3) The Master should obtain a receipt for the original bill of lading.

The receipt should be forwarded to the normal recipient of the cargo papers.

4.3.3. Letter of Indemnity

On tankers, a charterer may authorise the Master to release the cargo on presentation of a guaranteed letter of indemnity in lieu of bills of lading.

Cargo must not be released unless a telexed or written authority from Company Head Office, Charterer or B/L consignee is delivered to the vessel.

4.4. CHARTER PARTIES

4.4.1. Clauses

58

All charter parties contain many clauses designed to protect both the ship owner and the charterer.

The clauses vary from charter to charter and it is imperative that the Master is conversant with all of the clauses in any charter party his vessel is subject to, as failure to observe them in strict detail may well incur a penalty.

Charter parties are based on "standard" forms and made specific by "additional clauses" attached to the charter party these "additional clauses" are incorporated in and form part of the charter party.

The Master will be advised of "additional clauses" in excess of standard charter clauses in voyage orders.

4.5. DAILY WORKBOOKS

It is Company policy for the Chief Officers on all vessels to keep a daily record of all work carried out by their respective departments.

The records are to be retained on board and be available for inspection only by a Company officer.

4.6. OFF-HIRE REPORTING

Masters are required to report to the Company by the quickest means available during all/any off-hire periods.

The report must include the vessels position, time of off hire, reason for off hire, and the fuel and water ROB at the time when off hire commenced and when hire resumed.

4.7. DEEP SEA PILOT

It is Company policy to assist Masters wherever possible and any Master of a vessel who is either not familiar with the waters of a narrow channel or is unsure of the accuracy of available charts should contact Head Office in good time so that a pilot and/or charts can be arranged.

A list of pilot services available can be found in Port Information Books, Pilot Books & Radio Signals.

4.8. MARINE INCIDENTS

A casualty will be dealt with according to each Vessel's Emergency Response Plan/SOPEP and reported to the Company.

4.9. NOTES OF PROTEST

A 'Note of Protest' is simply a declaration by the Master of circumstances beyond his control which may give or have given exposure to loss or damage.

It is advisable for the Master to note protest in any of the following circumstances:

a) Whenever the vessel has encountered weather

conditions which may have resulted in damage to cargo or the vessel, or non-compliance with charter party clauses.

b)   When the vessel is damaged, regardless of cause.

c)   When it has not been possible to allow normal/required cargo ventilation due to adverse weather conditions.

d)   When cargo is shipped in such condition that it is likely to suffer deterioration during the voyage.

e)   When there is a discrepancy in the quantity of cargo loaded.

f)   When cargo loading/discharge has been delayed due to no fault of the vessel.

g)   When any breach of the charter party terms is committed by the charterer or his agent.

h)   When a consignee fails to discharge or take delivery of cargo.

i)   In all cases of general average.

Any protest issued against the vessel should be acknowledged "for receipt only and without prejudice".

4.10. STEVEDORE DAMAGE

The Officers of the Watch (OOW) must be constantly vigilant

at all times during cargo operations and immediately report any damage to the ship or cargo.

Written notice of any damage must be tendered to the stevedores at the earliest opportunity within 24 hours who must acknowledge receipt in writing. Wherever possible, damage caused by stevedores should be made good prior to departure.

Where stevedores refuse to accept receipt in writing a protest is to be issued and the matter treated as a dispute.

Any dispute should be reported to the Company office and a P&I surveyor called in if necessary.

4.11. NAVIGATIONAL WATCHKEEPING - GUIDANCE TO DECK OFFICERS

It is essential that the Officer of the Watch (OOW) appreciates that the efficient performance of certain duties is necessary in the interests of the safety of life and property at sea and the prevention of pollution to the marine environment.

The following guidance notes shall be observed at all times during the course of a routine navigational watch.

Nothing in this section removes from the Master his authority to take any steps and issue any orders, whether or not they are in accordance with the contents of the ship instruction manual, which he considers are necessary for the preservation of life, the safety of the ship and her cargo or for pollution prevention.

4.11.1 GUIDANCE TO DECK OFFICERS IN CHARGE OF A WATCH IN PORT

Arrangements for keeping a watch when the ship is in port shall:

a) Ensure the safety of life, ship, cargo and protection of the environment.

b) Observe international, national and local rules and regulations.

c) Maintain order and the normal routine of the ship.

d) Maintain safe access between ship and shore or ship and neighbouring vessel.

The Master shall decide the composition and duration of the watch depending on the conditions of mooring, type of ship and character of duties.

A qualified Deck Officer shall be in charge of the watch.

4.11.2. Taking over the Watch

The Officer of the Watch (OOW) shall not hand over the watch to the relieving officer if he has any reason to believe that his relief is not capable of carrying out his duties effectively; should this occur then he shall notify the Master.

The OOW shall pass the following information to his relief:

a) The depth of water at the berth, ship's draught, the level and time of high and low waters; condition of the moorings, arrangement of anchors and the scope of the chain, and other features of mooring importance for the safety of the ship, state of main engines and their availability for emergency use, the vessel's position at anchor along with relevant details of anchor bearings, landmarks, etc. and state of weather and expected forecast.

b) All scheduled work to be carried out on board. Full details of planned cargo and ballast operations in progress or to be started, current or future bunker operations, whether any craft are secured to the vessel, their purpose and if means of access has been granted to own vessel.

c) The levels in bilge, ballast and cargo tanks and the status of associated valves, pipelines, pumps and manifolds, as applicable.

d) The signals or lights being exhibited, correct national flags hoisted and any signal flags required by local rules or regulations.

e) The number of crew members required to be on board and the presence of any other authorised persons on board and the whereabouts of key personnel.

f)   The state of firefighting and lifesaving appliances.

g)   Any special port regulations.

h)   The Master's standing orders and special instructions

i)   The Chief Officer's standing orders and special instructions

j)   The lines of communication that is available between the ship and dock staff or port authorities in the event of an emergency arising or assistance being required.

k)   Other areas of importance affecting the safety of the ship and protection of the environment.

l)   Indicate which, if any, ship's side shell doors are open and in use and indicate the likelihood of further doors being required due to change in draft/trim/tide /gangway or for operational reasons.

m) Security of vessel particularly if vessel is in a known piracy area.   Number and position of ships security staff and any shore security personnel employed.

The relieving Officer shall satisfy himself that:

a)   The vessel is safely moored.

b)   The appropriate signals, lights and flags are properly hoisted and exhibited.

c)   Safety measures and fire protection regulations are being maintained.

d)   He is aware of the nature of any hazardous or dangerous cargo being loaded or discharged and the appropriate action in the event of any spillage or fire.

e)   No external conditions or circumstances endanger the ship and that his own ship does not endanger others.

If, at the moment of handing over the watch, an important operation is being performed, it should be concluded by the OOW and not his relief, except when ordered by the Master.

4.11.3. Keeping a Watch

The Officer of the Watch shall:

a)   Make rounds to inspect the ship at appropriate intervals paying particular attention to:

• The gangway height and security, anchor chain or moorings, especially at the turn of the tide or in berths with a large rise and fall and, if necessary, take measures to ensure that they are in normal working condition.

• The draught, under keel clearance and the state of the ship to avoid dangerous listing or trim during cargo handling or ballasting.

• Security/safety of shell door openings.

• Check that safety/security/fire patrols are being carried out on a regular basis.

• The vessel's air draught or trim at all times but especially during cargo handling bunkering or ballasting.

• The state of the weather and sea and forecasts.

• Observance of all regulations concerning safety precautions, fire protection and pollution prevention.

• Levels in bilges and tanks.

• All persons on board and their location, especially those in remote or enclosed spaces.

• The exhibition of any signals or lights, including flags.

• Funnel exhausts/smoke and advise the Engine Room accordingly.

b) In bad weather, or on receiving a storm warning, take the necessary measures to protect the vessel, personnel and cargo and inform the Master.

c) Take every precaution to prevent pollution.
Sight around the vessel to ensure that no pollution hazards exists.

d) In an emergency threatening the safety of the vessel, raise the alarm, inform the Master, take all possible measures to prevent any damage to the ship and, if necessary, request assistance from the shore authorities or neighbouring ships.

e) Be aware of the state of stability so that, in the event of a fire, the shore firefighting authority may be advised.

f) Offer assistance to ships or persons in distress as available without compromising the safety of his own crew or vessel.

g) Take all necessary precautions to prevent accidents or damage when propellers are to be turned.

h) Enter in the Deck logbook all important events affecting the ship and cargo operations.

4.11.4. Master's Standing Orders

The Master shall ensure that the watch keeping arrangements for the ship is at all times adequate for maintaining safe navigational and engineering watches.

The Master shall prepare standing orders for the deck officers responsible for navigating the ship.

These orders may simply refer to the duties and responsibilities mentioned below but must include any information/orders that the Master feels are necessary for any aspect concerning the safety of the crew, passengers, the vessel, the cargo and environmental protection which are specific to his ship.

The Master's Standing Orders *are to be signed* by all deck officers to ensure that they have been read and understood.

The Master's Standing Orders shall include, but not limited to, information on the following:

1) Maintaining a proper lookout

2) The bridge not to be left unattended

3) Course position and speed checked frequently

4) Use of all navigational equipment

5) Use of helm, engines and sound signals

6) When to notify the Master

7) Conditions for handing over the watch

8) Recording weather conditions and other activities

9) Checking of compass errors (frequency)

10) Procedure for changing from manual to auto steering and vice versa - instructions likely to be posted at changeover position

11) Requirement of Log entry for watertight openings

12) Procedure and requirements for reducing speed in heavy weather

4.11.5. Master's Night Order Book

The Master is required to enter written instructions to his navigating officers each evening when the vessel is at sea.

These instructions should be entered in the "Master's *Night Order* Book", this will ensure that the Master's navigational requirements will be known and agreed to by the OOWs.

4.11.6. Navigation

The intended voyage shall be planned in advance, taking into consideration all pertinent information, and any courses laid down shall be checked before the voyage commences.

During the watch the courses steered, position and speed shall be checked at sufficiently frequent intervals, using any available navigational aids necessary, to ensure that the ship follows the planned course.

The OOW shall have full knowledge of the location and operation of all safety and navigational equipment on board the ship and shall be aware and take account of the operating limitations of such equipment.

The OOW shall not be assigned or undertake any duties which

would interfere with the safe navigation of the ship.

4.11.7. Navigational and Positioning Equipment

The OOW shall make the most effective use of all navigational equipment at his disposal.

When using radar, the OOW shall bear in mind the necessity to comply at all times with the provisions on the use of radar contained in the International Regulations for Preventing Collisions at Sea, particularly with regard to keeping a proper visual and audio look out.

In cases of need the OOW shall not hesitate to use the helm, engines and sound signalling apparatus.

4.11.8. Periodic Checks of Navigational Equipment

Operational tests of shipboard navigational equipment should be carried out at sea as frequently as practicable and as circumstances permit,

In particular when hazardous conditions affecting navigation are expected,

Where appropriate these should be recorded in ship files.

The OOW should make regular checks to ensure that:

a) The helmsman or the automatic pilot is steering the correct course.

b) The standard compass error is determined every watch where possible; the standard and gyrocompasses are frequently compared, and repeaters are synchronized with their Master compass.

c) The automatic pilot is tested manually at least once a watch.

d) The navigation and signal lights and other navigational equipment are functioning properly.

e) The radar's performance is as noted in the Radar Logbook with regard to detection ranges.

f) Electronic position fixing systems are cross checked with other systems and radar/visual positions where available.

4.11.9. Navigational Duties and Responsibilities

The officer in charge of the watch shall:

a) Keep his watch on the bridge which he shall under no circumstances leave until properly relieved.

b) Continue to be responsible for the safe navigation of the ship, despite the presence of the Master on the bridge, until the Master informs him specifically that he has assumed that responsibility and that this is mutually understood.

c) Notify the Master when in any doubt.

d)   Not hand over the watch to the relieving officer if he has reason to believe that the latter is obviously not capable of carrying out his duties effectively, in which case he shall notify the Master accordingly.

On taking over the watch the relieving officer shall satisfy himself as to the ships estimated or true position and confirm its intended track, course and speed and shall note any dangers to navigation expected to be encountered during his watch.

He should also read, understand and sign the Master's Night Order Book.

A proper record shall be kept of the movements and activities during the watch relating to the navigation of the ship in the Bridge Logbook and/or Movement/Bell Book.

4.11.10. Look-out

In addition to maintaining a proper look-out for the purpose of fully appraising the situation and any risk of collision, stranding and other dangers to navigation, the duties of the look-out shall include the detection of ships or aircraft, shipwrecked persons, derelicts and debris. In maintaining a look-out the following shall be observed:

a)   The look-out must be able to give full attention to the keeping of a proper look-out and no other duties shall be undertaken or assigned which could interfere with that task.

The look-out must be qualified in accordance with the requirements stated in relevant Merchant Shipping Notices or other appropriate publications.

b)   The duties of the look-out and helmsman are separate, and the helmsman shall not be considered to be the look-out while steering. The OOW may be the sole look-out in daylight provided that on each such occasion:

i)   The situation has been carefully assessed and it has been established without doubt that it is safe to do so.

ii)   Full account has been taken of all relevant factors including, but not limited to:

• State of the weather and visibility
• Traffic density
• Proximity of any danger to navigation
• The attention necessary when navigating in or near traffic separation schemes

c)   Assistance is immediately available to be summoned to the Bridge when any change in the situation so requires.

4.11.11. Navigation in Coastal Waters

The largest scale chart on board, suitable for the area and corrected with the latest available information, should be used.

Fixes should be taken at frequent intervals. Whenever circumstances allow, fixing should be carried out by more than one method.

The OOW should positively identify all relevant navigation marks.

4.11.12. Clear Weather

The OOW should take frequent and accurate compass bearings of approaching ships as a means of early detection of any risk of collision.

Such a risk may sometimes exist even when an appreciable change in bearing is evident, particularly when approaching a very large ship or a tow or when approaching a ship at close range.

He should also take early and positive action in compliance with the applicable Regulations for Preventing Collisions at Sea and subsequently check that such action is having the desired effect.

The use of radar in this context is quite acceptable and perhaps preferable when the OOW is an experienced radar observer who fully understands the principles of plotting.

4.11.13. Navigation in Fog

Sensible use of radar and other modern aids to navigation has greatly assisted the conduct of ships in fog, but these aids have not reduced the need to comply fully with the Collision Regulations, i.e.:

To proceed at a safe speed, pay special attention to good watch-keeping and navigate with proper caution.

To post extra lookouts and maintain a watch by sight and hearing,

The Board of the Company stresses the need for prudent navigation in fog and all Masters and Officers must be aware of any limitations in the performance of the vessel's radar and other navigational aids.

The guidance contained in Merchant Shipping Notices and other appropriate publications shall be followed whenever practicable.

4.11.14. Navigation in Ice

Ice should be regarded as a considerable obstacle to a vessel's progress and great care must be exercised. Before encountering ice in any form, careful passage planning must be observed.

This should include the Master discussing with all the Navigating Officers the procedures to be followed when the vessel first encounters the ice edge. Additionally, the draft and trim of the vessel, the immersion of the propeller and the rudder need to be taken into consideration.

Masters should obtain the latest ice information available by all means at their disposal, including an assessment of the density and thickness of the ice and plot on the chart the location of the ice edge together with changes in the strength and direction of the wind since receipt of the latest report.

The importance of keeping a continuous lookout when approaching the ice edge cannot be too strongly emphasised.

This visual lookout together with a radar lookout is recommended but the limitations of radar in detecting ice must be recognised.

4.11.15. Navigation with Pilot Embarked

Notwithstanding the duties and obligations of a pilot, his presence on board shall not relieve the Master or the OOW from their duties and obligations for the safety of the ship.

After his arrival on board, in addition to being advised by the Master of the manoeuvring characteristics and basic details of the vessel for its present condition of loading and given a pilot card, the pilot must be fully supported by the ship's bridge team.
Masters and Deck Officers must be aware of the dangers associated with hydrodynamic interaction.

Attention is drawn to the following extract from IMO

Resolution A 285 (VIII):

'Despite the duties and obligations of a pilot, his presence on board does not relieve the OOW from his duties and obligations for the safety of the ship.

He should co-operate closely with the pilot and maintain an accurate check on the vessel's position and movements.

If he is in any doubt as to the pilot's actions or intentions, he should seek clarification from the pilot. And if doubt still exists, he should notify the Master immediately and take whatever action is necessary before the Master arrives.'

4.11.16. Pilot Boarding Arrangements

The International Maritime Pilots' Association requirements for the boarding arrangements of a pilot are displayed on a chart included in the ICS Bridge Procedures Guide and are defined in the current SOLAS regulations.

Where embarkation/disembarkation involves the use of a helicopter the guidance in the ICS Guide to Helicopter/Ship Operations on Marine Pilot Transfer Communications and Ship Operating Procedures should be followed.

4.11.17. Calling the Master

The OOW should notify the Master immediately in the following circumstances:

a)   If restricted visibility is encountered or expected.

b)   If the traffic conditions or the movements of other ships are causing concern.

c)   If difficulty is experienced in maintaining course.

d)   On failure to sight land, a navigation mark or to obtain soundings by the expected time.

e)   If, unexpectedly, land or a navigation mark is sighted or an unexpected change in soundings occurs.

f)   On the breakdown of the engines, steering gear or any essential navigational equipment.

g)   In heavy weather if in any doubt about the possibility of weather damage.

h)   If the ship meets any hazard to navigation, such as ice or derelicts.

i)   In any other emergency or situation in which he is in any doubt.

j)   At any other time as noted in the Master's Orders

Despite the requirement to notify the Master immediately, the OOW should, in addition, not hesitate to take immediate action for the safety of the ship where circumstances so require.

4.11.18. Watch keeping Personnel

The OOW should give watch keeping personnel all the appropriate instructions and information to ensure the keeping of a safe watch including an appropriate look-out.

4.11.19. Ship at Anchor

If the Master considers it necessary, and/or local regulations require, a continuous navigational watch should be maintained at anchor.

In all circumstances, while at anchor, the OOW should:

a) Determine and plot the ship's position on the appropriate chart as soon as the vessel is at anchor and "brought up",

Check at sufficiently frequent intervals whether the ship is remaining securely at anchor by taking bearings of fixed navigation marks or readily identifiable shore objects,

The correct use of radar in this context is quite acceptable.

b) Ensure that an efficient look-out is maintained.

c) Ensure that inspection rounds of the ship are made periodically.

d) Observe meteorological and tidal conditions and the state of the sea.

e) Notify the Master and undertake all necessary measures if the ship drags anchor.

f) Ensure that the state of readiness of the main engines and other machinery is in accordance with the Master's instructions.

g) If visibility deteriorates, notify the Master and comply with the applicable Regulations for Preventing Collisions at Sea.

h) Ensure that the ship exhibits the appropriate lights and shapes and that appropriate sound signals are made at all times, as required.

i) Take measures to protect the environment from pollution by the ship and comply with applicable pollution regulations.

j) Monitor VHF channel 16 and others as per local regulations and Lists of Radio Signals for the reception of weather, traffic and other information.

4.12. FIRE, PREVENTION AND CONTROL

4.12.1. Co-operation with Port and Public Fire Brigades

Ship to shore communications should be reviewed to ensure that they provide the quickest possible contact with the port/public fire brigade at all times.

A fire plan should be placed at the point of access to the

vessel and up-to-date stability information, cargo plans and a crew list should be immediately available.

Any local regulations regarding firefighting equipment readiness, positioning and availability are to be complied with.

4.12.2. Fire Fighting Appliances

At all times water supplies of adequate pressure should be immediately available on board, either in the ship's fire main or in hoses run on board from other sources.

Extra apparatuses such as adapters for hose couplings and foam making appliances should always be available and the deployment of any additional apparatus considered necessary for the particular ship should not be left until there is an outbreak of fire.

Any fire appliances removed for repair or recharging should be replaced at once with similar appliances.

The possibility that the ship's power supply to fire detection or protection systems may fail or become disconnected must be taken into account.

On tankers, immediately before or on arrival at the terminal to load or discharge cargo, the ship's fire hoses should be connected to the fire main, one forward and one aft of the cargo manifold.

If practicable a pump should maintain pressure on the ship's fire main while cargo or ballast is being handled.

If this is not possible the fire pump should be in a standby condition and ready for immediate operation.

In cold weather, freezing of fire mains and hydrants can be avoided by continuously bleeding water overboard from hydrants at the extreme ends of each fire main. Alternatively, all low points of the fire main may be kept drained.

Foam monitors should be ready for use. Portable fire extinguishers, preferably of the dry chemical type, should be conveniently placed near the ship's manifold.

A check should be made to confirm that both ship and shore have an International Shore Fire Connection for the transfer of water for firefighting. Terminal firefighting appliances should also be ready for immediate use.

4.12.3. Stability

When firefighting operations endanger a ship's stability and it is necessary to decide whether firefighting should cease, the decision of the Harbour Master or other responsible officer of the port authority, after consultation with all interested parties, should prevail.

However, this does not relieve the Master, or in his absence the officer-in-charge from bringing to the notice of the fire brigade any special circumstances affecting the safety of the ship, its stability, or the conduct of fire-fighting operations.

4.12.4. Machinery Availability

While a tanker is berthed at a terminal, its boilers, main engines, steering gear and other machinery essential for manoeuvring should normally be maintained on stand-by to enable the ship to move away from the berth at short notice.

Repairs and other work which may immobilise the vessel should not be undertaken at a berth without prior written agreement with the terminal.

It may also be necessary to obtain permission from the local port authority before carrying out such repairs or work.

4.13. WARNING NOTICES

All safety notices must be clearly visible to all personnel working on board the vessel, particularly those on the pump room access.

All notices must also display the appropriate symbols in accordance with SOLAS regulations.

Notices containing the following warnings should be posted near the gangway on berthing or near the accommodation ladder when the vessel is at anchor.

WARNING
NO NAKED LIGHTS
NO SMOKING
NO UNAUTHORISED PERSONS

4.14. SMOKING

Smoking should be permitted only under controlled conditions.

There may however be occasions when, due to the nature of the cargo being transferred or other factors, a total prohibition of smoking may be necessary.

The designated smoking places on a tanker or on shore should be agreed in writing between the Master and the terminal representative before operations start.

On dry cargo vessels No Smoking areas should be clearly marked.

The Master is responsible for ensuring that all personnel on board are informed of the selected places for smoking and for posting suitable notices.

On tanker vessels certain criteria should be followed in the selection of smoking places whenever petroleum cargoes are being handled or when ballasting, inert gas freeing and tank cleaning operations are taking place.

• The agreed smoking places should be confined to locations abaft the cargo tanks

• The agreed smoking places should not have doors or ports which open directly on to or over the cargo deck or on to decks overlooking cargo spaces or shore connections.

• Account should be taken of conditions that may suggest danger, any indication of unusually high petroleum gas concentrations, particularly in the absence of wind, and when there are operations on adjacent tankers or on the jetty or berth.

• In the designated smoking places all ports should be kept closed, and doors into passageways should be kept closed except when in use.

• The air conditioning should be put on full recirculation.

4.15. MOORINGS

Vessels are to be securely moored and kept alongside during loading and discharging.

Holding a ship in position alongside is the responsibility of the ship's staff.

The best way to stay in position is by carefully planning and arranging the mooring layout when berthing.

4.16. COLD WEATHER PRECAUTIONS

The Master must take all necessary precautions to prepare the ship for operation during periods of very cold weather.

All departments must be familiar with the precautions to be taken to avoid damage under these circumstances.

4.16.1. Cargo Systems

a) To prevent return drains freezing between the return and steam manifolds on fore deep tanks, a small jumper line must be installed.

b) Cargo heating returns, main lines and coils must be cleared of water/moisture by air blowing if they are not in use.

c) Before freezing weather sets in and until anticipated return to a warmer climate, keep steam on heating coils if their use is anticipated.

d) To keep moisture out of 'dry use' lines, all return and steam valves must be tightened and tested.

4.16.2. Fittings and Piping in Machinery Spaces

a) Where space heaters exist, use them to maintain a suitable operating temperature for machinery.

b) Keep all water systems circulating

4.16.3. Bunkers

Cold weather boiler demands can increase fuel consumption.

Bunker reserves must be higher when cold weather or operation in ice is anticipated.

4.16.4. Deck Machinery and Piping

a)   The Chief Engineer must be advised well before expected cold weather and kept advised of actual temperatures.

b)   When cold weather is expected at sea prior to departure, have winches greased and ready to turn over slowly when steam is turned on as temperatures approach freezing.

Ensure that steam/exhaust line bypasses are open to allow steam into the exhaust piping.

c)   Keep watch on winches to assure continuous rotation.

Painting stripes on winch drums will help in noting the slow rotation.

d)   Water filled inert gas overpressure relief devices, where fitted, should have antifreeze added and maintained at the correct mixture.

4.16.5. Emergency Generator Fuel Tank and Emergency Fire Pump

a) To be sure of adequate fuel and to reduce condensation in the tank, keep tanks at least 90% full.

b) Take necessary measures to prevent fuel waxing.

c) If the emergency diesel engine is not in a heated compartment, the jacket water system and radiator should have antifreeze added.

4.16.6. Strainers, Sea Suction and Heat Exchangers

a) Where possible have less than three feet of trim to prevent ice from sliding under the vessel and reaching the sea suctions.

Steam or air injectors to sea suctions should be tested prior to arrival in ice.

b) Whenever possible, keep sea suctions and propeller below the ice level by proper ballasting procedures.

Vessels with 'high' and 'low' suctions should use the 'low' suctions in ice.

c) If possible, maintain deepest draft by loading cargo prior to discharging ballast.

d) If sea chests and/or suction piping get ice clogged, they should be thawed with Butterworth equipment or steaming out fittings.

Have adequate feed water reserves available.

4.16.7. Plating, Cargo and Ballast

a)   In heavy ice flow, the ship should be docked with the bow stemming the ice flow.

Avoid anchoring in these conditions if possible.   When berthed in a tidal flow use of main engines at minimum RPM, with terminal permission, may be required to break up ice around the stern and to prevent the vessel being "wedged" of the berth by ice.

b)   When underway in heavy ice, astern operation should be minimal, but if essential the rudder should be kept amidships.

Use minimum power ahead to keep steerageway.

c)   Checks for possible hull plating damage must be made after every heavy ice transit, by carefully inspecting all empty spaces.

The same inspections should be made in very cold weather after hard impacts with docks, pilings, fenders, etc.

d)   Before entering a cold climate ballast water should be exchanged for clean seawater if possible when passing through a warm current.

4.16.8. Weather Deck Piping

a) Put steam on the pump rooms if required for cargo operations. Otherwise the pump room exhaust and steam piping should be drained.

b) Sanitary systems and soil lines must have continual restricted water flow.

To help preclude freezing, flush meters can be selectively tied down and unused drain traps can have antifreeze added.

c) All unused piping should be blown dry after draining, including:

• Tank(s) vent systems

• Wash and potable water filling systems

• Forecastle head educator system

• Compressed air lines

• Fire mains.

In circumstances where fire mains must remain pressurised, ensure sufficient flow of water to prevent freezing by bleeding water off through suitable connections (e.g. hawse pipe washing connection and stern hydrants).

4.16.9. Other Precautions

a) Decks must be kept free of ice.

b) Keep fresh water outboard tanks slack as sea water temperatures approach 32°F (0°C). In severe weather air pipes to ballast tanks must be checked clear prior to ballasting/de-ballasting to avoid the possibility of a tank collapse.

c) Keep outside doors closed as much as possible.

d) Watch for and repair steam or water leaks.

e) Check for the possibility of flooding from ruptured piping in pump room bilges, shaft tunnels and other remote spaces.

f) Keep space heaters available for use in 'dry' storage areas where condensation can collect and freeze.

g) Keep electronic equipment ON or on STANDBY to ensure that heating elements are on. Careful reading of the equipment's operating manuals will be required.

4.17 POLLUTION PREVENTION IN PORT

Masters, Officers and Ratings are required to take all reasonable practicable steps to prevent pollution of the environment by:

- Oil
- Dangerous Goods and Harmful Substances
- Sewage
- Garbage

- Organisms in Ballast Water
- Exhaust and Cargo Vapour Emissions.

4.17.1 Reporting

Pollution Incidents similar to those described in this section must be immediately reported to the office.

In addition to reporting all pollution incidents, Masters are required to record and report all near miss occurrences that may have resulted in pollution to enable the Emergency Response Team to investigate, collate, analyse and subsequently implement recommendations as necessary.

4.17.2 Oil Pollution

The reporting formats for oil pollution and when, how to report are contained in the vessel's approved Shipboard Oil Pollution Emergency Plan.

The SOPEP is to be used by all vessels, operating world-wide.

All tankers operating in the waters of the USA **MUST** use the USCG approved Vessel Response Plan.

4.17.3. Inadequacy of Reception Facilities for Oil Residues

The Master of a ship faced with a lack of reception facilities, or reception facilities which are not adequate, for any of these categories of waste should submit directly to the

Company appropriate details of the inadequacy on the report form annexed to M1390. The Company will then inform the Marine Safety Agency in UK.

The MSA will evaluate each report received and, where in its opinion the allegation of inadequate facilities is justified, it will:

i)   In the case of non-UK ports inform the flag state of the alleged inadequacy and also inform, where applicable, the IMO Secretariat by means of annual summary reports; and

ii)   In the case of UK ports take up the matter of the alleged inadequacy directly with the port and terminal concerned.

When possible, it would be helpful to those providing reception facilities if, before making such a report, the Master brought the alleged inadequacy to the attention of the harbour authority or terminal operator concerned.

He would then only need to make a report if the problem could not be resolved at the time.

4.17.4. Discharge of Sewage

Raw sewage must not be discharged from a holding tank unless the vessel is more than 12 miles from land and underway.

Sewage from an approved commuting and disinfecting system must not be discharged unless the vessel is more than 4 miles from land.

Liquid sewage from vessels with a sewage treatment plant of approved specification can be discharged less than 4 miles from land but the sludge must be discharged at least 12 miles from land.

Extreme care must be taken to ensure that, when sewage is being discharged, there is no likelihood of the effluent entering the sea water inlets for freshwater generators.

If there is any possibility of this occurring, then the FW generator must be stopped whilst discharge of the sewage tank is in progress.

4.17.5. Disposal of Garbage

The permitted discharge into the sea of various types of garbage is defined in MARPOL 73/78, Annex 5.

It should be noted that plastics may not be discharged anywhere at sea and consequently plastic wrappings must be separated and retained for disposal ashore or incinerated on-board.

Several incidents have arisen where the Owner/Master has been fined for disposing of garbage contrary to the MARPOL regulations either by disposal in a prohibited area or incorrect garbage transfer/handling procedures.

4.17.6. Garbage Disposal Record Book

In keeping with the MARPOL regulations, all vessels are provided with a Garbage Disposal Record Book which must log the disposal of all garbage whether at sea or in port.

The book must be available for inspection if required by any authorised surveyor.

Additional copies of the book are available from the Company.

4.17.7. Ballast Water

Organisms carried in the ballast water in vessels that have ballasted in certain areas are believed to present a hazard to environmentally sensitive areas when ballast water is discharged.

Presently the main country which has enacted legislation relating to the discharge of ballast water is Australia.

However, some U.S. states have made similar or more stringent regulations.

The following recommendations are made:

a) Ballasting should be avoided in shallow or turbulent water.

b) Ballast water should be exchanged, preferably in open tropical water, but not within, or adjacent to, Australian territorial waters.

Similar procedures apply to some U.S. states whilst others require that all segregated ballast on-board that cannot be discharged ashore is to be discharged before entering waters within the jurisdiction of the state.

The Company is aware that item a) above may be difficult to comply with and that item b) may impose unacceptable stresses on the vessel and consume fuel oil.

Logbook entries should be made whenever any operation regarding ballast is carried out to comply with ballast water legislation.

The polluting organisms are mainly carried in the sediment in ballast water tanks and, where stability requirements permit, ballast tanks should not be stripped dry whilst the vessel is in Australian territorial waters.

In the case of U.S. ports where states require discharge of ballast ashore:

a) If segregated ballast cannot be discharged to shore it should be discharged to sea and ballast taken into tanks or holds that can be discharged ashore.

b) Where ballast cannot be taken into tanks or holds that can be discharged ashore it should be reduced to a minimum amount to be retained on-board prior to arrival, commensurate with local regulations, weather conditions, stress and stability limitations and safe navigational practices.

4.17.8. Bilge Water

Bilge water can only be discharged in accordance with the requirements of MARPOL 73/78, as amended.

4.17.9. Exhaust Emissions

Funnel emissions are strictly monitored in some countries - most notably in Japan and the USA.

The following general precautions should be taken:

a)   Soot blowing in port should be avoided.

b) The Deck OOW should advise the Duty Engineer whenever smoke is seen emitting from the funnel.

c)   When initially starting the main engine, a watch should be kept, and the engine room notified if smoke or sparks are evident.

d)   If an occasion arises where an unavoidable emission of dark smoke is foreseen, prior notice should be given to the Port Authorities whenever possible.

4.17.10. Garbage Pollution Initial Report Format

Extreme caution must be observed at all times while the vessel is transiting any prohibited area.

However, should an incident occur which cannot be rectified

(e.g. garbage landing in dock water which is not retrievable), an initial report must be forwarded to the Company containing the following information:

a) Name of ship, call sign, and flag.

b) Date and time of incident (specify GMT or local).

c) Whether vessel is at sea or within port jurisdiction (indicate port).

d) Vessel's position.

e) Brief details of incident.

- This should include details of garbage and total amount, how it is packaged, garbage handling procedures in place at time of dumping

- Reason for inadvertent dumping

- Witnesses to incident both crew and shore and estimated movement of garbage

f) Shore officials contacted by vessel/agents.

g) Is litigation likely?

h)   Media involvement or is there a likelihood?

Vegetable oils or fats must be disposed of in the correct manner so as not to cause a pollution hazard. Fat fryers and skillets holding oil requiring disposal are not to be poured down sinks/scuppers with the possible risk of entering the vessel's sewage tanks or directly over side.

All vegetable oils are to be drained into clearly marked metal containers labelled 'Waste Food Oils' and disposed of ashore.

4.18. PRE-SAILING PROCEDURES

4.18.1. Introduction

It is a legal requirement that before any vessel proceeds to sea it must be in every respect in a seaworthy condition and capable of reaching its intended destination.

A note to this effect must be entered in the Deck Logbook.

To comply with this condition certain criteria must be met and at any port a government official can with-hold permission to depart should the vessel in his opinion be deficient of any of the following.

4.18.2. Charts and Passage Plan

Charts for the intended passage must be corrected to the latest information available together with relevant light lists, pilot books, etc. taking into account that the vessel may be required to proceed via a routing services advised route.

4.18.3. Stability

The vessel's stability must be calculated and recorded, with the sailing condition available for inspection and a copy forwarded to head office.

It is recommended that the sailing condition and cargo/ballast distribution are kept with the Vessels Response Plan.

4.18.4 Bunkers

Bunkers must be sufficient for the intended passage with a suitable safe margin.

4.18.5. Drafts Recorded

The departure draft must be recorded and made available to all interested parties together with the dock water density.

4.18.6. All Cargo Secured

An entry is to be made in the deck logbook confirming that the Chief Officer has checked the securing of all cargo and any lashing arrangements are satisfactory.

On tankers all valves are to be closed after the vessel's personnel are satisfied that there can be no movement of cargo on the forthcoming voyage.

The vessel must be made watertight by the closing and proper securing of hatches, sounding pipes manholes, etc.

Due regard should be paid to ventilators which may or may not be required to remain open.

4.18.7. Deck Equipment Stowed

Derrick and cranes for cargo, hose handling and stores are to be properly stowed and secured.

4.18.8. Loose Equipment Above and Below Decks

A check is to be made that all loose equipment, oil drums, gas bottles are adequately secured with proper lashings and not temporary chocks.

4.18.9. Crew

A full crew as required by the minimum safe manning certificate must be on board prior to departure or the vessel will be considered unseaworthy.

Any missing crew members must be reported to the shore authorities and the appropriate action taken.

4.18.10. Stowaways & Drugs

A search for stowaways and drugs must be carried out prior to departure with the result of the search being recorded in the logbook.

4.18.11. Bridge Gear Tested

"Bridge gear tested" is not an acceptable entry in the deck and engine logbooks.

Each item tested must be specified as required in the Company Standing Instructions, with any defect noted and reported.

The Bridge Department Checklist should be stapled to the relevant page of the Deck Logbook.

4.18.12. Weather

The weather forecast for the imminent period after departure should be available to the Master obtained from the vessel's radio equipment, vessel's agency or port authority.

For vessels departing in a ballast condition the anticipated weather conditions will influence the quantity of ballast taken.

4.18.13. Pilotage and Tugs

If used, pilots and tugs are usually ordered by the vessel's agency, and to avoid cancellation or detention expenses prompt attention to all items listed in the pre sailing procedures will prevent the vessel not being ready for departure at the anticipated time.

Pilot embarkation and disembarkation arrangements must be checked by a competent person.

4.18.14. Pre-Departure / Pre-Arrival Checklist

The Company's pre-departure and pre-arrival checklist forms are to be completed.

Officers of the Watch must refer to the Master's Standing Instructions for any specialised equipment requiring testing during departure and arrival procedures.

4.18.15. Verification of Crew/ Numbers

Prior to departure (after shore leave expires) the head of each department will report to the Master that all his crew are on board including and supernumeraries

4.19. AFTER SAILING

4.19.1. Mooring Equipment

Immediately after departure all mooring equipment is to be secured and protected.

Anchors are to be secured with locking bars in position.

Spurling pipes are to be covered and cemented to prevent the possibility of shipping water into the chain locker when the vessel has cleared the port.

Storm plates should be set in place over the upper ends of the hawse pipe.

4.19.2. Scuppers

Scuppers can be unplugged only when it has been determined that the decks are free of oil and oily material.

Occasionally, due to sailing with a restricted draft, it is necessary soon after departure to transfer bunkers.

If the transfer is via deck mounted pipelines scuppers should remain plugged until the transfer is complete.

4.19.3. Oil Record Book

The Oil Record Book should be complete with all relevant signatures.

4.19.4. Bills of lading

Any discrepancy between the quantity and condition of cargo stated on the bills of lading and the quantity and condition of cargo calculated to be on board is to be telexed to head office immediately together with details of any notes of protest issued or received.

4.20. PASSAGE PLANNING

4.20.1. Responsibility for Passage Planning

The Second Officer is responsible for preparing detailed passage plans to the Master's requirements prior to departure.

In those cases when the port of destination is not known or is subsequently altered, it will be necessary for the Second Officer to extend or amend the original plan as appropriate.

The passage plan must cover the period from departure berth on departure to arrival berth (when known) and not just pilot to pilot passages.

4.20.2. Principles of Passage Planning

There are four distinct stages in the planning and achievement of a safe passage:

1.   Appraisal
2.   Planning
3.   Execution
4.   Monitoring

These stages must of necessity follow each other in the order set out above.

An appraisal of information available must be made before detailed plans can be drawn up and a plan must be in existence before tactics for its execution can be decided upon.

Once the plan and the manner in which it is to be executed have been decided, monitoring must be carried out to ensure that the plan is followed.

All Masters and Officers are required to follow the guidance contained in ICS Bridge Procedures Guide, and adopt the principles of passage planning.

4.21. LOGBOOKS (DECK, ENGINE AND OFFICIAL)

The general instructions for completing the deck logbook are printed inside the front cover.

Each entry in the logbooks must be completed in ink and any error should be crossed out with a single line and initialled.

If logbooks are completed in duplicate the original must always remain on board.

The copy will be despatched to the company.

4.22. CHARTS AND NAUTICAL PUBLICATIONS

It is the Master's responsibility to ensure that all necessary charts and publications for the vessels trading area are on board.

All charts and publications on-board are to be corrected with the charts and publications for the anticipated voyage being corrected first.

The Master must ensure that the Second Officer keeps the vessel's outfit of charts and publications up to date with the latest editions of the weekly Notices to Mariners and that chart correction certificates are returned to the office.

Working charts should be ready for immediate use together with the relevant tide tables, pilot book, list of lights and list of radio signals.

Chapter 5: Familiarization with the Cargo Operations

The vessels technical superintendent should be acquainted with the relevant regulations for the carriage and handling of the various types of cargo and knows that it is the Master's duty to ensure that all crew follow the Code of Safe Working Practices for Merchant Seamen.

To cover all cargoes in this chapter, you should know that the attention of Masters and Officers are focused on the IMDG Code, CSWPMS, CHRIS code and stability hazards.

5.1. CARGO OPERATIONS

Once the vessel is secured at a berth and prior to any cargo operations, the Master must discuss fully with the Chief Officer and Shore Representatives.

• Local Rules

• Type of Cargo and associated hazards and dangers

• Sequence of Loading/Discharging

• Hatch Quantities

• Stress/Stability/Draughts

• Watch and Shift Arrangements

• Emergency/Pollution Procedures

5.1.1. Lifting Plant Winches Cranes and Derricks

All vessels are required to complete register of ships lifting appliances and cargo handling gear which must be available for inspection prior to any cargo operations requiring the use of the vessel's equipment.

Although a record of inspection is required annually, it is the Masters duty to ensure that at all times all lifting plant and associated gear is kept in good working order with regular routine inspection.

5.1.2. During Loading and Discharging Operations

Any observed misuse of the vessel's cargo handling equipment by stevedores must be reported immediately.

Any lifts by two or more appliances simultaneously can create hazardous situations and should only be carried out where necessary - they should be properly conducted under the close supervision of a responsible person after thorough planning of the operation.

Wire ropes should be regularly inspected and treated with the Company specified lubricants.

These should be thoroughly applied so as to prevent internal corrosion as well as corrosion on the outside.

The ropes should never be allowed to dry out.

The requirement for maintenance means that the lifting plant should be kept in good working order, in an efficient state and in good repair.

Systematic preventive maintenance should be undertaken, with due account taken of any manufacturers' instructions, which should include regular route inspection by a person who is competent to assess whether the lifting plant is safe for continued use.

These inspections should be at intervals related to the character and usage of the plant.

Safety devices fitted for lifting appliances should be checked by the operator before work starts and at regular intervals thereafter to ensure that they are working properly.

5.2. CRANES AND DERRICKS

Ships' cranes and derricks should be properly operated and maintained in accordance with
Manufacturers' instructions and the Masters should ensure that sufficient technical information is available including the following:

a) Length, size and safe working load of falls and, where appropriate topping lifts.

b) Safe working load of all fittings.

c) Boom limiting angles and SWL.

d) Manufacturers' instructions for replacing wires, topping up hydraulics and other maintenance as appropriate.

A mass in excess of the safe working load should not be lifted unless:

a) A test is required.

b) The weight of the load is known and is the appropriate proof load.

c) The lift is a straight lift by a single appliance.

d) The lift is supervised by the competent person who would normally supervise a test and carry out a thorough examination.

e) The competent person specifies in writing that the lift is appropriate in weight and other respects to act as a test of the plant, and agrees to the detailed plan for the lift.

f) No person is exposed to danger thereby.

Before a derrick is raised or lowered, all persons on deck in the vicinity should be warned so that no person stands in, or is in danger from, bights of wire and other ropes.

All necessary wires should be flaked out.

Before any attempt is made to free equipment that has become jammed under load, every effort should first be made to take off the load safely.

Precautions should be taken to guard against sudden or unexpected freeing.

Others not directly engaged in the operation should keep in safe or protected positions.

5.2.1. Code of Hand Signals

Refer to CSWPMS for correct signals.   All crew on deck must be aware of the stop signal. During use of cranes and derricks only a designated person should make the required signals, except in an emergency.

5.3. HATCHES

The Master shall ensure that a hatch covering shall not be moved unless it can be removed and replaced, whether manually or with mechanical power, without endangering any person.

The Master shall ensure that a hatch shall not be used unless the hatch covering has been completely removed, or if not completely removed, is properly secured.

No person shall operate a hatch covering which is power-operated unless authorised to do so by a responsible ship's officer.

5.3.1 General

Weather deck hatch covers, and their securing arrangements should be inspected at regular intervals.

All hatch covers should be properly maintained, and defective or damaged hatch covers should be replaced or repaired as soon as possible.

Damaged or defective covers should not be used, particularly during loading or unloading.

All covers and beams should only be used if they are a good fit and overlap their end supports to an extent which is adequate but not excessive.

All weather deck hatch covers should be kept in a weather tight condition when closed.

They should be handled with care; at all times when hatches are open, the area around the opening and in the hatchways should be appropriately illuminated and guard rails rigged.

Lifting appliances where used should be able to be attached to hatch covers from a safe position and without a person being exposed to danger of falling or being trapped.

Loads should not be placed over or works take place on, any section of hatch cover unless it is known that the cover is properly secured and can safely support the load.

Each member of the crew involved with the handling of hatch covers on the vessel should be properly instructed in their handling and operation.

All stages of opening or closing hatches should be supervised by a ship's officer or other experienced person.

No hatch covering should be replaced contrary to information showing the correct replacement position.

Hatch covers should not be used for any other purpose.

5.3.2. Mechanical Hatch Covers

The appropriate manufacturer's instructions with respect to the safe operation, inspection, maintenance and repair of the type of mechanical hatch cover fitted should be complied with in all respects.

During operations, all persons should keep clear of the hatches and the cover stowage position and the area should be kept clear of all items which might foul the covers or the handling equipment.

Special attention should be paid to the trim of the vessel when handling mechanical covers. The hatch locking pins or preventers of rolling hatch covers should not be removed until a check wire is made fast to prevent premature rolling when the track way is not horizontal.

Hatch wheels should be kept greased and free from dirt; the coaming runways and the drainage channels kept clean. The rubber sealing joints should be properly secured and be in such a condition as to provide a proper weather tight seal.

The coaming compression bar should be free of damage, scaling and or distortion.

All locking and tightening devices should be secured in place on a closed hatch at all times when at sea. Securing cleats should be kept greased and correctly adjusted. Cleats, top-wedges and other tightening devices should be checked regularly whilst at sea.

Hatch covers should be properly secured immediately after closing or opening.

They should be secured in the open position with chain preventers or by other suitable means.

No one should climb on to any hatch cover unless it is properly secured.

5.3.3. Non-Mechanical Hatch Covers and Beams

Each non-mechanical hatchway should be provided with an appropriate number of properly fitting beams and hatch covers, pontoons or slab hatches adequately marked to show the correct replacement position, and with an adequate number of properly fitting tarpaulins, batten bars, side wedges and locking bars so that the hatch will remain secure and weather tight for all weather conditions.

Unless hatches are fitted with coamings to a height of at least 760 mm (30 inches) they should be securely covered or fenced to a height of 1 metre (39 inches) when not in use for the passage of cargo.

Manually handled hatch covers should be capable of being easily lifted by two men.

Such hatch covers should be of adequate thickness and strength and provided with hand grips.

Wooden hatch boards should be strengthened by steel bands at each end.

Hatch boards, hatch beams, pontoon hatches, hatch slabs and tarpaulins should be handled with care and properly stowed, stacked and secured so as not to endanger or impede the normal running of the vessel.

One man should not attempt to handle hatch covers unaided unless the covers are designed for one-man operation.

Hatch boards should be removed working from the centre towards the side and replaced from the sides towards the centre.

When hauling tarpaulins, seamen should walk forward and NOT backwards so they can see where they are walking.

A derrick or crane being used to handle beams, pontoons or slab hatches should be positioned directly over them to lessen the risk of violent swinging once the weight has been taken.

Appropriate gear of adequate strength should be specially provided for the lifting of the beam's pontoons and slab hatches.

Slings should be of adequate length, secured against accidental displacement while in use and fitted with control lanyards.

The angle between arms of slings at the lifting point should not exceed 120°, in order to avoid undue stress. The winch or cranes should be operated by a competent person under the direction of a ship's officer or other experienced person.

Beams and hatch covers remaining in position in a partly opened hatchway should be securely pinned, lashed, bolted or otherwise properly secured against accidental dislodgement.

Hatch covers and beams should not be removed or replaced until a check has been made that all persons are out of the hold or clear of the hatchway.

Immediately before beams are to be removed, a check

should be made that pins or other locking devices have been freed.

No one should walk out on a beam for any purpose.

Hatch covers should not be used in the construction of deck or cargo stages or have loads placed on them liable to damage them.

Loads should not be placed on hatch coverings without the authority of a ship's officer.

5.3.4. Steel-Hinged Inspection/Access Lids

Inspection/access hatch lids should be constructed of steel or similar material and hinged so they can be easily and safely opened or closed.

Those on weather decks should be seated on watertight rubber gaskets and secured weather tight by adequate dogs, side cleats or equivalent tightening devices.

When not secured, inspection/access hatch lids should be capable of being easily and safely opened from above and, if practicable, from below.

Adequate hand grips should be provided in accessible position to lift inspection/access hatches by hand without straining or endangering personnel.

5.3.5. Cargo Ramps and Ship Side Doors

Cargo ramps and ship side doors must only be opened whilst the vessel is alongside under the supervision of a responsible officer.

Before opening ships, side doors or cargo ramps safety rails should be fitted across the opening until a safe access has been rigged.

Accesses ways must always be fitted with handrails and where appropriate a safety net.

With ship side openings, access via openings is not permitted until proper safe access has been rigged by ship's crew.

With cargo ramps, no movement of vehicles, etc. should be allowed until the foot walkway is properly guarded, and ramp handrails have been fitted.

Whilst ramps and ship side doors are open, sealing and securing arrangements must be checked by the Chief Officer and Chief Engineer and any deficiencies made good whilst the vessel is alongside.

Immediately prior to departure from a berth, all ramps and ship side doors are to be checked by the Chief Officer or Chief Engineer and a positive report made on the doors being closed and properly secured.

5.4. BULK CARGOES

The IMO Code of Safe Practice for Solid Bulk Cargoes contains information in respect of materials carried in bulk and recommendations in respect of safety, cargo distribution, and cargoes which may liquefy under certain conditions.

Masters are required to ensure that a copy of the latest edition of the IMDG Code is retained on board.

5.4.1. Cargo Procedures

The purpose of this section is to serve as a reminder to ships' personnel and ship and terminal operators of the need to observe essential precautions and routines before and during cargo loading or unloading operations.

It is essential that the Master and Senior Officers are familiar with the contents of the IMO Code of Safe Practice for Solid Bulk Cargoes (BC Code).

The SOLAS Convention requires that information on the cargo to be loaded must be provided to the Master by the shipper. Section 4 of the BC Code gives guidance on the type of information to be expected, thus allowing proper assessment of its carriage to be made.

Masters should insist that adequate information is always made available; the safety of the ship depends upon it.

A detailed loading plan must always be prepared. In large bulk carriers several passes must be made, loading part of the cargo for each hold on each pass. The use of a loadicator will allow comprehensive calculations to be made, and thereby ensure that the number of passes is sufficient not to overstress the ship.

If, during the loading operations, difficulties or problems are experienced that may cause significant departures from the stresses allowed for in the plan, then cargo loading should be suspended.

When discharging cargo, especially if impact methods are used to dislodge residues, the possibility of damage to the ship's structure exists.

Even minor distortions or fractures, when repeated in many places in several hold, will have a cumulative effect upon the overall strength of the ship.

Masters should be alert to the risk of potential damage by such practices and should intervene if necessary.

The Master must ensure ship's personnel constantly monitor the cargo operation to confirm the agreed plan is being followed.

This will include regular checks of the draught to confirm tonnage figures supplied, and both should be recorded in a cargo logbook.

If significant deviations are detected, cargo operations should be suspended, and a safe plan calculated to correct the matter before resumption is allowed.

A written agreement must be submitted by a shipper accepting responsibility for the discharge of cargo overloaded should his equipment or personnel fail to stop loading when requested to do so.

5.4.2. Ship/Shore Safety check List

The Master and the terminal operator should complete the checklist jointly.

The safety of operations requires that all questions should be answered affirmatively.

If an affirmative answer is not possible, the reason should be given, and agreement reached upon appropriate precautions to be taken between ship and terminal.

If a question is considered to be not applicable, a note to that effect should be inserted.

5.4.3. Provision of Cargo Information

While overall responsibility must lie with the Master, the IMDG Code requires him to be provided with written information relating to the characteristics and condition of the cargo.

The responsibility of providing this information rests with the shipper.

5.4.4. Carriage of Dangerous Goods

While the IMDG Code recommends the need for strict observance when loading cargoes in bulk which may shift or flow during the voyage, it must also be borne in mind that there are many substances which are dangerous to load in bulk no matter how they are secured against movement, either because of their chemical content or their inherently dangerous properties.

For this reason, it is unlawful, by virtue of Reg 14 of the Merchant Shipping (Dangerous Goods) Regulations 1981 to load such goods in bulk and it is the duty of the owner, his servant or agents to ascertain whether or not specific goods can be carried safely in bulk. Recommendations to be closely followed are contained in "The Carriage of Dangerous Goods in Ships".

5.4.5. Duties of the Master

It is the Masters duty prior to loading any cargo to ensure that:

a) The stability and stress for the intended loaded condition of the ship is based on the information contained in the ships approved stability book and will be within "limits" throughout the voyage.

b) The bilges are clean and empty, strum boxes are clear, and the pumps and bilges have been tested.

c) That proper information regarding the cargo, treatment, packaging and hazards associated with the cargo are provided by the shipper.

5.4.6. Precautions on Entering Cargo Spaces

Certain cargoes are known to absorb oxygen, particularly organic and natural ore cargoes, from the atmosphere and may emit flammable, narcotic or toxic fumes.

It is therefore important to ascertain whether the cargo behaves in this manner and if such possibilities exist.

The cargo space should not be entered until it has been opened out and adequately ventilated and the enclosed space entry procedures followed.

5.5. COAL CARGOES

The principal aim of this Section is to remind those engaged in the carriage of coal of the dangers associated with the emission of flammable gases and spontaneous combustion and to provide advice on means to reduce the risk of such dangers.

5.5.1. Dangers which can arise

a) Emission of Flammable Gases:

All grades of coal will emit methane, an odourless flammable gas which is less dense than air.

A methane/air mixture containing between 5 per cent and 15 per cent methane constitutes an atmosphere which can be readily ignited by sparks or naked flames (e.g. electrical or frictional sparks, a match, or lighted cigarette, etc.) to produce a highly dangerous and potentially lethal explosion.

Although a methane/air mixture containing more than 15 per cent methane is not explosive itself it could, after dilution with air, become explosive and therefore should also be regarded as hazardous.

b) Spontaneous Combustion:

Spontaneous combustion can occur with certain types of coal. Reaction with oxygen causes the temperature of the coal to rise to a point at which self-ignition occurs and burning commences.

Should spontaneous combustion occur, a deep-seated fire may develop, and a very difficult, dangerous situation can arise.

5.5.2. Precautionary Measures

The dangers outlined above can be minimised and possibly eliminated if the following safeguards are carefully observed.

Safeguards applicable to the ship

a) Bulkheads and decks forming the boundaries between

the cargo compartments and any accommodation space, any other enclosed space which can be used by the crew or shore personnel (e.g. deck store rooms, workshops, pump rooms, cofferdams, duct keels, forecastle, tweens, etc.) or any machinery space, shaft tunnel, chain locker, or similar space, should be gas-tight.

b) All reasonable measures should be taken to prevent gases emitted from the cargo accumulating in the adjacent enclosed spaces referred to above (e.g. avoid placing access hatches or other openings to cargo compartments in such spaces, ensure that ventilation trunks from the cargo compartments are in sound structural condition and gas-tight whenever they pass through any enclosed space, etc.).

Where for sound practical reasons this cannot be done special arrangements should be made (e.g. hold access from within a mast house or deckhouse should be in a separate space with its own ventilation). In all such cases warning notices should be prominently displayed on the entry door.

c) All the enclosed spaces referred to above should be provided with efficient means of ventilation; which in the case of such spaces as cofferdams, chain lockers, etc., may be provided for by means of access openings.

d) Steps should be taken to prevent any gases which may be emitted from the coal cargo from entering any other cargo compartment not being used for the carriage of coal.

e) All coal cargo compartments should be provided with

effective surface ventilation to remove any explosive or flammable gas which might accumulate above the surface of the coal cargo.

Ventilation may be by natural or mechanical means and when conditions permit, assisted by the partial opening of hatch covers.

On no account should the arrangements be such that air can be directed into the body of the coal as this could promote spontaneous combustion.

The arrangements should provide only for surface ventilation and any openings which provided ventilation to the lower parts of the cargo space should be blanked off before loading commences.

At all times the Master shall:

a) Prohibit smoking, the use of naked flames or welding in the cargo and adjacent areas unless satisfied that all spaces where flammable gases may accumulate have been properly ventilated.

b) Ensure that, weather permitting, all cargo spaces are effectively ventilated.

c) Prevent personnel from entering any enclosed space in which methane might accumulate or via a non-gastight access hatch or doorway, etc. until it has been thoroughly ventilated.

The guidance given in Chapter 10 of the Code of Safe Working Practices for Merchant Seamen should be followed.

d) Obtain temperature readings of the cargo and gas readings of the hold/compartment at intervals not exceeding 12 hrs.

5.5.3. Spontaneous Combustion

It may be possible to detect the development of spontaneous combustion by regularly taking temperatures in the cargo compartments.

However, coal is a bad conductor of heat and the failure to detect any hot areas in the stow should not be taken as a sign that spontaneous combustion is not taking place in areas not accessible for the taking of temperatures.

Use should be made of any suitable pipes or trunks passing down through the holds from the deck to take temperatures but digging into the body of the coal is not recommended.

To minimise the risk of explosion due to methane emission even when spontaneous heating is suspected, ventilation of the spaces above the cargo, which may in emergencies include limited opening of hatch covers, should continue until there is clear evidence that the cargo is burning.

At this stage the aim would be to contain the fire in the cargo hold and to achieve the Master should:

a) Ensure that the cargo compartment is completely closed down against the entry of air.

b) Apply carbon dioxide, inert gas or high expansion foam into the hold if these are available.

c) Use water to cool the boundaries of the cargo space but water or steam should never be applied directly to the burning coal.

d) Monitor hold bulkhead, deck-head temperatures and gas emissions from holds.

e) Ensure that the space remains sealed until the ship reaches port and specialist advice followed concerning the precautions necessary, including the time when it would be safe to open hatch covers and work the cargo.

5.5.4. Cargo Stability

The danger of the cargo shifting will be minimised provided that it is stowed and trimmed in all directions as reasonably level as is practicable and the TML is within "limits".

5.5.5. Slurry - Duffs - Small Coals and Coke

The principal aims of this Notice are to remind those engaged in the carriage of coal of the dangers associated with those types of coal cargoes which can in certain circumstances liquefy. It is also to provide advice on precautions to reduce the risk of such dangers.

Under the stimulus of ship motion and vibration a coal cargo liable to liquefy can cause progressive listing and eventual capsizing.

The following types of cargoes can in certain circumstances liquefy:

- Coal slurry

- Coal duff

- Coal duffs containing particles greater than 50 mm

- Small coal

- Coke.

Before a ship sails, it is essential that the average moisture contents of the cargo shall not exceed the transportable moisture limit of the coal.

5.5.6. Check Testing

Where, despite care in protecting the cargo after testing, there is some suspicion that a part may have absorbed further moisture; check testing should be carried out as follows:

5.5.6.1 Shipboard Moisture Test for Average Moisture Content

If the circumstances are such that a laboratory test cannot be made of the cargo about to be loaded and a suitable drying oven and weighing scale are available on board ship, then the moisture content of a representative sample of the cargo about to be loaded may also be determined in the specified manner by shipboard test (see IMO Code Appendix D (D1.1.4.4).

The result should be compared with the certificate of flow moisture point provided by the Supplier or Shipper.

5.5.6.2 Shipboard Test for Possibility of Flow

On board ship, or at the dockside, the following procedures for approximately determining the possibility of flow may be used to check a sample with a top size less than 7 mm.

Half fill a cylindrical can of approximately half a litre with a sample of cargo.

Take the can in one hand and bring it down sharply to strike a hard surface such as a solid table from a height of 200 mm.

Repeat the procedure 25 times at one or two second intervals.

If water appears on the surface of the sample, it is a clear indication that the cargo is unsafe.

This test is of limited value, however, since the non-appearance of water is not necessarily an indication that the cargo is safe; it therefore does no more than confirm that the cargo is not safe, and should never be used to determine whether or not a cargo may be loaded without proper testing and sampling.

5.5.7. Duties of the Master

In deciding whether or not a particular coal cargo is safe to carry, the Master should regard the following:

Prior to Loading the Master shall:

a) Carefully note the contents of information from the Shippers so any test results which appear suspect (e.g. by virtue of moisture testing having taken place some days previously, or by virtue of the flow moisture point having been determined at a previous date or for a previous batch) should be questioned.

On the basis of the information provided the Master should be satisfied that the cargo is safe for shipment.

b) Note that pending the issue of the moisture certificate it is permissible to commence loading of the part of the cargo which has been sampled and tested provided the Master is satisfied that the average moisture content of the cargo will not exceed the transportable moisture limit.

c) Ensure that the stability of the intended loaded condition of the ship, based upon the information contained in the ship's Approved Stability Information Booklet, will comply with the standard of stability required for the assignment of load line and that this will be maintained throughout the voyage.

d) Be satisfied that the bilges are clean and empty, the strums or rose boxes are clear and that limber boards, where fitted, are intact.

The pumps and bilges should be tested prior to loading.

e) In some ports it is customary to dampen the coal to prevent dust, etc. during loading. The Master should try to obtain representative samples of the cargo and obtain an analysis of the moisture content.

Where doubt exists, the Master should reject the cargo until the physical condition of the cargo is proved safe.

During and after loading, the Master shall ensure that:

a) As loading the cargo has been trimmed into the wings as far as is reasonable and practicable and where necessary into the ends of the compartments.

b) During wet weather all openings should be closed weather-tight immediately upon completion of loading and when not in use.

c) The cargo hold bilges are regularly pumped to remove any water which may collect. The quantity of water removed from each hold must be recorded.

5.6. IRON AND STEEL CARGOES

5.6.1. General

Whilst proper care must be taken with the stowage of all iron and steel, cargoes of pig iron, steel billets, round bars and pipes are particularly difficult to secure effectively.

In the upper 'tween decks of many two and three deck ships, the absence of hatch coamings more than a few inches high adds to the difficulty of securing pig iron and billets carried abreast the hatchways and there appears to be a greater risk of cargo shifting in these spaces than in the lower holds.

The most effective way to secure these cargoes is to level them and over-stow them with other suitable cargo.

The over stow should be of sufficient rigidity or weight to act as a positive preventative to the movement of pig iron, steel billets, bars, etc.

Large quantities of uncovered pig iron or billets should not be carried in the upper 'tween decks in order to reduce the righting lever and make the vessel less "stiff" since this does not eliminate the risk of cargo shifting and may endanger the ship if it does shift.

5.6.2. Pig Iron

When pig iron is not spread over the whole of the

compartment and is not effectively secured by other suitable cargo, it should be stowed at a uniform level in bins which may be formed by the bulkheads, the ship's side, hatch coamings of at least its own height, and either fore and aft or traverse shifting boards.

The shifting boards should be very robust in view of the weight they will have to support during heavy rolling.

They should be not less than 3 inches think and should rise slightly above the level of the pig iron.

They should be supported by steel uprights about 5 feet apart consisting of 5-inch angle bars well bolted at the top and bottom or secured in some equally efficient manner.

Planking, toms and shores should be effectively secured.

They should not merely be jammed in place.

Whenever "glossy finished" pig iron, which has a smooth machine-cast finish, is carried it should be loaded on wood ceiling and well levelled out into the wings of the holds. If it is carried in 'tween decks or superstructures it should be stowed in bins, similar to those described in the paragraph above, and there should be a strong middle line bulkhead.

This bulkhead should rise to a height of 1 foot above the surface of the pig iron.

5.6.3. Steel Billets

When cargoes of steel billets in ocean-going ships are not effectively over-stowed, it is recommended that the precautions should be taken, especially when the cargo is carried in the tween decks.

Attention is also drawn to the difficulties in achieving a safe stow when the billets are irregularly shaped and to the need to ensure that the stow is being made secure as loading progresses, if necessary, at each layer.

In addition, when irregular shaped billets are to be shipped attention should be paid to the provision of information relating to shape and stowage factor in advance of shipment.

5.6.4. Ingot Moulds, Steel Coils (Coils of Sheet Steel)

The need for great care in stowing and securing cargoes of steel coils,

The coils should whenever possible, be stowed in regular tiers from side to side of the vessel making maximum use of pillars, centre line bulkheads, etc.
Except when special provision has been made for stowing coils on end, they should always be stowed on the round, with each coil being stowed and against its neighbour, and with wedges of dunnage being driven well home under the rounds.

The final coil to be stowed in each row will normally rest on the cantlines of the two adjacent coils as the space remaining will normally be less than the diameter of a coil.

The weight of this coil will lock the other coils in the row in position.

This coil should be lashed to the two coils supporting it.   If it is necessary to load a second layer over the first, then it should be stowed in the cantlines of the first tier; wire lashings should be placed over each row of coils in the top layer.

The stow should be further secured by using wire lashings to secure coils together and to lash each row back to the bulkhead from which the stow commenced.

Single shores should not be relied upon but should be held in place by a secondary shores or lashings.   Rigging-screws should be included at suitable positions in all lashings and access during sea passage for inspection and attention should be possible.

Where a space between coils is unavoidable, ample small timber should so be placed that any movement in the coils will cause the timber to "settle" and make a solid stow.

Similar precautions should be taken in securing ingot moulds or any other heavy objects.

5.6.5. Round bars and Pipes

Level out from side to side is not in itself sufficient to prevent shifting of round steel bars or similar cargoes.

It is recommended that additional precautions should be taken to secure such cargoes firmly against shifting by using wires adequately set up and by careful "tomming".

5.6.6. Steel Plates

Steel plates stowed either singly or in bundles may shift if unsecured, and so may heavy pieces of steel (or other weighty materials) if stowed upon steel turnings or other insecure foundations.

These cargoes are inherently prone to slip over decks, other cargoes or their own surfaces.

When they move because of ship motion this occurs suddenly and re-stowage at sea is unlikely to be possible.
Such movement can rupture a vessel's side as well as produce a list.

When not stowed within a compartment where they are locked by the boundaries and adjacent timber spacing, they should be independently secured by chain or wire lashings as well as by "tomming".

5.6.7. Steel Scrap

Particular care needs to be exercised during the loading of steel scrap to minimise the possibility of a shift of cargo causing a list, or a movement of a heavy piece of scrap causing damage to the ship's structure. The former can occur due to a collapse in the stow if heavy scrap is loaded over lighter material, if voids are left in the wings or ends of the compartment, or if a compact stow is not achieved.

Damage caused by the movement of a piece of heavy scrap with sharp corners or edges can include the piercing of the ship's side plating below the waterline with consequential flooding.

Every effort should be made during loading to achieve a level and compact stow with the absence of voids.

In addition, heavy pieces of scrap which could cause damage to the ship's structure if they were to move should be adequately over-stowed or secured by the most appropriate means.

5.6.8. Heavy Coils of Steel Wire

Coils are to be held tightly together and substantial securing arrangements are to be used.

Where spaces between the coils are unavoidable or where there are spaces at the sides or ends of the compartment substantial "tomming"" should be used.

Where this is not practicable, the spaces should be solidly packed with timber or other un-damageable cargo.

In addition, the coils should be secured with wire lashings, provided, where appropriate, with rigging screws.

One alternative to the method of stowage, is to stow each coil on the flat in the cantlines of the adjacent coils in the tier.

The coils in successive tiers can be stowed so that each coil overlaps a number of coils below instead of being stacked in columns.

Unavoidable spaces at the sides and ends and between coils should then be secured as suggested above.

When two different types of steel cargo are being stowed in the same compartment, and it is necessary to stow one on top of the other, consideration should be given to the ability of the lower consignment to support the upper one to avoid the former settling or collapsing and causing the latter to shift.

Due regard should of course also be paid to the provision of adequate transverse stability when the upper cargo is of a denser nature.

5.7. LOADING OF TIMBER DECK CARGOES CARGO LASHING - SLIP HOOKS

Because of the frequency with which casualties involving timber deck cargoes still occur, it is necessary to emphasise the importance of complying with The Merchant Shipping (Load Line) (Deck Cargo) Regulations 1968 and with the IMO publication "Code of Safe Practice for Ships Carrying Timber Deck Cargoes".

Masters are reminded of the importance of using slip hooks or other cargo-securing appliances of a satisfactory type and maintaining them in good condition.

Examples of defects in this respect have been slips made of iron which broke at the welds and slip hooks designed with straight tongues, in consequence of which tension on the lashings tended to force the securing rings into the release position and a slight jar on the fittings released them.

In examining the lashing of timber deck cargoes, Masters should be aware of the dangers arising from the jamming of slip hooks; fittings, etc. during a voyage and should take precautions to ensure that this does not occur.

One solution would be to use additional slip hooks, in the overall lashings, so arranged as to reduce the chances of jamming, for instance by arranging them back to back.

Attention should be drawn to the danger of ship's personnel inherent in the jettisoning of deck cargo should this become necessary.

An assessment of the situation might under certain circumstances indicate that the jettisoning operation would be accomplished more safely with the aid of a system of additional temporary lashings sited such that the final release can be made from a safe position.

5.8. WOOD PULP

Experiments have confirmed that it is possible for saturated wood pulp to exert sufficient pressure to lead to the complete rupture of the boundaries of the compartments in which it is stowed.

It is therefore essential that the upmost care should be taken to prevent the entry of water into spaces containing this cargo.

In particular, all air pipes and ventilators to compartments containing wood pulp should be effectively closed against accidental admission of water and protected against damage by deck cargo.

5.9. GRAIN CARGO

Masters are reminded of their statutory responsibilities to ensure that every ship in which they are involved, and which is to carry grain fulfils two basic requirements:

a)   It has been issued with, and carries on board a document of authorisation.

b)   The grain is properly loaded in accordance with the regulations as described in the document of authorisation.

5.9.1. Stowage

Masters are advised to check that the apparent volume occupied by the grain up to the top of the grain in the hatchway is approximately the same as the volume obtained by multiplying the weight of the grain loaded by the stowage rate for the type of grain. If the apparent volume is appreciably greater than the volume calculated from the stowage rate, it must be assumed that there are voids in the hold and steps should be taken to eliminate them.

It is essential for every ship that the shipper should provide the Master with an accurate stowage rate for the grain before it is loaded into the ship.

In many ports, grain is fumigated after loading by sealing hatches and adding chemicals.

The chemicals added are toxic to humans and daily monitoring of hatch seals is vital.

The ship's Officers must check the type of fumigants used and be aware of fire hazards associated with types and or age of fumigants used. Fumigated hold entrances must be marked with appropriate hazard warnings and crew briefed of hazard.

5.10. CONTAINERS

Masters should be aware of the inherent dangers when containers and flats are carried in ships not specially constructed or effectively modified for the carriage of such cargo units, if they are not adequately secured against movement.

Masters should satisfy themselves in this regard for all containers and flats, whether stowed on or below deck before the ship leaves her berth. They should not accept units for loading, which, from external inspection, they consider to be structurally un-safe or large units which would result in an overhang of the ship's side.

Refrigerated containers should be running as soon as possible after loading so that the Chief Engineer may confirm the refrigeration unit is in good working order.

Carriage temperature should be provided in writing by the shipper.

Containers carried on deck should be stowed preferably fore and aft, prevented from sliding athwart ships and securely lashed against tipping.

At no time should deck-loaded containers overstress the hatch covers or the hatchway structure.

In cases of doubt, details of load and stress limitations should be obtained from the Classification Society.

Securing of containers and flats should be by means of chains, wires or other equally effective arrangements, in each case provided with means of tensioning.

Deck fittings should be so located that there will always be a good lead for securing arrangements.

It is not sufficient, however, to ensure the security of the unit itself in the ship; particular regard should also be paid to the security of the cargo stowed on flats.

Heavy metal cargoes products, vehicles and farm implements are some of the more difficult cargoes and there are particular problems with bulky cargoes stowed in polythene bags.

It cannot be emphasised enough that it should never be assumed that cargo which has been loaded on flats which may arrive at the port covered by tarpaulins, is adequately secured for a sea passage.

It is particularly important that Masters obtain an accurate Cargo Stowage Plan showing the distribution of weights and in addition, details of the contents of any cargo units containing dangerous goods.

It is also important that due regard be paid to prevailing, forecast, and anticipated weather conditions during the voyage.

Cargo units which contain dangerous goods must be marked with the appropriate identification label. Guidance on packing is given in the IMO/ILO Guidelines for Packing of Cargo in Freight Containers and Vehicles (MSC Circular 383)

Satisfactory means in the form of guard rails, lifelines, walkways or gangways, etc. should be provided for the protection of the crew in getting to and from their quarters, the machinery space, and all other parts used in the necessary work of the ship.

If fore and aft access cannot be gained on the deck because of inadequate width to the side of containers, safe and efficient access should be arranged over the top of the cargo.

The Merchant Shipping (Load Lines) (Deck Cargo) Regulations 1968 relate to the safe stowage of deck cargoes and the provision of safe access for the crew.

Failure to observe the requirements under these Regulations renders a Master liable to proceedings under the Merchant Shipping (Load Lines) Act 1967.

General guidance on the carriage of containers on deck is also given in Chapter 28 of the Code of Safe Working Practices for Merchant Seamen.

5.11. HAZARDOUS CARGOES (IMDG CODE)

Modern cargo handling procedures, including the development of container transport, have significantly reduced the risk of pollution in recent years.

However, certain substances, including dangerous goods carried in packaged form, will give rise to pollution damage to the marine environment if packages are damaged and the contents released into the sea.

Such cargoes are designated as harmful substances under Annex III of MARPOL 73/78 and identified as marine pollutants in the International Maritime Dangerous Goods (IMDG) Code.

Dangerous goods carried in packaged form, or in solid form in bulk, are covered by the requirements of Part A, Chapter VII of SOLAS 1974, as amended.

Detailed provisions giving effect to the statutory requirements of SOLAS are set out in the Code of Safe Practice for Solid Bulk Cargoes (BC Code). This publication is incorporated into the Supplement to the IMDG Code, Section 3.

5.11.1. Group Emergency Schedule (EmS)

The handling and transport of dangerous goods shall be carried out by the safest means and with the greatest care, in order to prevent pollution incidents as well as contamination of other cargoes and/or vessel's stores.

It is essential that those personnel involved in the handling and transportation of dangerous goods are advised beforehand of the characteristics and hazardous properties of any hazardous goods and of all necessary safety precautions to be observed. They shall also be provided with information about safety rules, first aid treatment, emergency procedures to be followed and action to be taken in case of an incident.

Emergency procedures have been specially prepared in the form of recommendations contained in the supplement to the IMDG Code, providing Masters with advice on the immediate action to be taken should an incident involving hazardous goods occur.

These procedures are grouped so that substances or articles with the same or similar emergency action appear together on one emergency schedule (EmS).

The recommended emergency procedures and actions refer to substances, materials and articles listed in the IMDG Code; they must be followed in conjunction with the information provided in the IMDG Code and the Medical First Aid Guide for Use in Accidents Involving Dangerous Goods (MFAG).

5.12. CARGO PILFERAGE

During loading and discharging operations the deck watch patrol should make every effort to prohibit cargo pilferage, reporting any observed to the Chief Officer or shore security.

Chapter 6: Familiarization with the Standard Dry dock Repair Specifications

Ship Technical Superintendent is responsible to prepare the ship for entering to the dry docks for repairing, and he is responsible to prepare all work repair specification according to:

- Classification societies survey schedule and reports
- Engines running hours
- Dry docking intervals schedule
- Any damages on-board during the operation

This chapter will help you to prepare the dry dock repair specifications.

6.1. General Services

"You should to start the repair specification with the general services which required for your ship."

In your repair specification you can write the following:

- All general services, whether in original specification or as additional, shall be verified by the owner's representative.

- Unauthorized general services shall not be accepted.

- The yard must arrange and provide all necessary services, as long as the ship is alongside or inside the dry dock, until all repair work is completed, and the ship is sailing.

- These services are as follows:

  - Fire and Safety watchman each day.
  - Garbage skips each day.
  - Electrical shore power connection and disconnection.
  - Electrical shore power per unit (KW).
  - Temporary connection of fire main to ship's system.
  - Maintaining pressure to ship's fire main each day.
  - Sea circulating water (cooling line) connection.
  - Sea circulating water (cooling) each day.
  - Telephone connection on board ship.
  - Supply of ballast water per connection.
  - Supply of fresh water per connection.
  - Connection and disconnection of compressed air.
  - Gas-free testing per test/visit and issue of gas- free certificate.
  - Electric heating lamps per connection.
  - Ventilation fans and portable ducting each crane use per hour.

6.2. Hull Preparation

"You should know that the charges for the hull preparation works are given in price per square meter.

Also, you should be clear the job in your specification by submit the technical data of hull preparation such as hull divisions, hull area, paint application and painting material data sheet, type of blasting"

As soon as the dock is dry, the yard has to carry out the following:

- Remove hull fouling (scraping) immediately.
- High pressure washing (fresh water) and degreasing.
- Hull inspection by the yard, paint inspector, and ship superintendent for blasting area agreement prior to commencement of blasting.
- All ship's side valves, speed log, echo sounder, and any other external sensors are to be suitably protected prior to commencement of blasting.
- Propellers are to be protected prior to commencement of blasting.
- No application of blasting is to be made until the protections of the above mention are approved by the superintendent.
- Blasting is to be started as per an area agreement.
- Low pressure washing (fresh water) after blasting and prior to commencement of painting.
- No application of paint is to be made until hull service preparation is approved by superintendent and paint inspector.

- Technical data, such as thickness, over coating time, drying time before undocking, etc., must be adhered to.
- Application of paint will be under supervision of superintendent and paint inspector.
- Hull marking (draft marks, load line, ship names, IMO, port home, etc.).
- Paint owner supply.

Types of Hull Preparation

- Hand scraping normal
- Hand scraping hard
- Degreasing before preparation works
- High pressure jets wash
- Hydro blast
- Soda blast
- Vacuum dry blast
- Grit blast
- Grit sweep
- Grit blast to Sa 2
- Grit blast to Sa 2.5
- Spot blast to Sa 2.5
- Hose down with fresh water after dry blast
- Disc preparation to St2

Hull Painting Division Area

- Flat bottom

- Vertical sides
- Topsides

6.3. Rudder Works

As soon as the dock is dry, the shipyard has to carry out the following:

- Staging to be erected and removed after rudder works is completed.
- Rudder plug to be opened for checking of water in rudder.
- Air test is to be carried out if necessary; if any cracks are found, these are to be repaired.
- Rudder clearances are to be measured under the supervision of the ship's chief engineer.
- Handing over the report to the superintendent immediately.
- Pintels access to be removed for interior cleaning, inspection, and clearance measure.
- Repacking of stock gland (packing owner supply).
- MPI & dye check used as per superintendent instruction.
- Remove old zinc anodes and fit new ones (owner supply).

6.4. Propeller Works

As soon as the dock is dry, the yard must carry out the following:

- Staging to be erected and removed after repair work is completed.
- Rope guard to be removed and refit after repair work and testing are completed.
- Wear down to be measured in top and bottom under supervision of ship's chief engineer.
- Handing over the report to the superintendent immediately.
- Polish the propeller blades (face and back) and cover with grease.
- Propeller hub and blades dye check used as per superintendent instructions.
- Zinc anodes fitted on outer shaft seals to be checked and replaced as per superintendent instructions (owner supply).

6.5. Tail Shaft Withdrawal Works

As soon as the dock is dry, the yard has to carry out the following:

- Disconnection and removal of the propeller and landing in dock bottom.
- Disconnection and removal of tapered, keyed, and inboard tail shaft coupling.
- Drawing tail shaft outboard and landing in dock bottom for survey, cleaning, calibrating.
- Magna flux (MPI) testing of tail shaft taper and keyway, refitting all on completion.
- Disconnection of inboard intermediate shaft, flanged

couplings, releasing one in number journal bearing holding down bolts.

- Rigging intermediate shaft, lifting clear, and placing in temporary storage on ship's side, withdrawing tail shaft inboard.
- Hanging in accessible position, cleaning, calibrating, and refitting on completion.
- Relocating intermediate shaft and journal bearing in original position, fitting all holding-down bolts and recoupling flanges - all done as before.

6.6. Tail Shaft Simplex Seals Works

As soon as the dock is dry, the yard must carry out the following:

- Disconnection and removal of forward and aft seal liners.
- Removing ashore to workshop.
- Fully opening it up.
- Cleaning for examination and calibration.
- Reassembling with new rubber seals from owner's supply.
- Excluding all machining works.

6.7. Cathodic Protection Works

As soon as the dock is dry, the yard must carry out the following:

- Cut off existing anodes as per superintendent

instructions.

- Refit the new anodes (owner supply) as per owner marking the locations.
- Protect any anodes prior to commencement of painting.
- Anodes protection to be removed after painting is completed.

6.8. Sea Chests Works

As soon as the dock is dry, the yard must carry out the following:

- Staging to be erected and removed after work required is completed.
- Sea chest grids to be opened for cleaning and washing.
- Blasting as per an area agreement.
- Painting as per paint maker instructions and as approved by superintendent.
- Cut off existing zinc anodes as per superintendent instructions.
- New zinc anodes to be fitted (owner supply).
- Zinc anodes to be protected prior to commencement of painting.
- Zinc anodes protection to be removed after superintendent approval.
- Sea chest grids to be closed after completion.

6.9. Bottom Plugs

As soon as the dock is dry and when directed by the superintendent, the yard must carry out the following:

- Bottom plugs to be opened and checked as marked by ship's staff.
- Any plug needing renewal must be renewed through a new job order.
- Any block needing shifting to enable the opening of the plug must be done through a new job order.
- Bottom plugs are to be closed and tested after completion.

6.10. Sea & Side Storm Valves Works

The yard must carry out the following:

- Valves to be opened in situ as marked and listed by ship's chief engineer.
- Valves to be cleaned, lapped, repacked, and painted.
- Valves spindle, gland, disk, and other items to be checked.
- Valves to be inspected by superintendent and ship's chief engineer.
- Valves to be closed after superintendent approval.
- Any fabrications or spars supply must be done through a new job order.
- Any valve needing to be completely overhauled in the workshop must be done through a new job order.

6.11. Fenders Repairs

As soon as the dock is dry, the yard must carry out the following:

- Staging to be erected and removed after repair work is completed.
- Marking of damaged fender to be carried out in presence of ship's superintendent.
- Cropping existing damaged fender, hand grinding remaining edges, and preparing remaining flat hull plating for welding.
- Supply and fit new fender in half-round standard schedule 80 steel pipe with full fillet welding fender in place.
- Paint to be applied.

6.12. Bilge Keel Repairs

As soon as the dock is dry, the yard must carry out the following:

- Staging to be erected and removed after repair work is completed.
- Marking of damaged bilge keel to be carried out in presence of ship's superintendent.
- Cropping existing damaged bilge keel, hand grinding remaining edges and preparing remaining flat hull plating for welding.
- Supply and fit new bilge keel and weld in place.
- Paint to be applied.

6.13. Anchors & Chains Works

As soon as the dock is dry, the yard must carry out the following:

- Anchor chains (P&S) are to be lowered and ranged in dock bottom.
- Both chains are to be washed and cleaned.
- Both chains are to be calibrated and a report handed over to the superintendent.
- Both chains are to be joined end to end.
- Both chains studs are to be inspected.
- Mark all shots with paint and wires.
- After confirming anchor swivel and pin are free, lift up prior to undocking.

6.14. Chain Lockers Works

As soon as the anchor chains are ranged in dock bottom, the shipyard must carry out the following:

- Both chain lockers manholes are to be opened.
- Both chain lockers are to be cleaned and have mud removed.
- Both chain lockers are to be washed; pump out washing water after washing.
- Superintendent inspection.
- Both chain lockers are to be painted as per superintendent's instruction.
- Manhole is to be closed after superintendent approval.

6.15. Steel Repairs

Marking off the damaged area of hull plating is to be carried out according to UTG drawings in the presence of ship's superintendent:

- Cropping by hand burning and removal of all cropped plating.
- Dressing and preparation of plate edges of remaining external plating.
- Dressing and preparation of remaining internal structure.
- Supply and preparation of new steel plating, blasting to Sa2.5 and applying one coat of holding primer.
- Transport of new plate to vessel, fitting up, wedging in position, minor fairing and dressing of plate edges in the immediate vicinity, applying first runs of welding on one side, back gouging from other side and finally filling and capping to give fully finished weld.
- NDT to be carried out.

6.16. Pipe Works

According to listed pipes by C/E, the yard must carry out the following:

- Removal of existing pipe and disposal ashore.
- Fabrication of new pipe in workshop to pattern of existing one complete with new flanges.
- Pipe pressure test to be carried out.
- Delivery on board of new pipe and installation in place with supply of new jointing, bolts, and nuts.

- Refit of original clamps with new bolts and nuts.

6.17. Mechanical Works

6.17.1. Main Engine - Piston Withdrawal

According to engine running hours record & class inspection plan, the yard must carry out the following:

- Open up cylinder cover.
- Remove piston.
- Clean under scavenging space, smoothen cylinder liner in way of ports and collar.
- Test cylinder L.O. System by hand operating.
- Renew piston rings (owners supply) and smoothen up rings edges.
- Check piston top clearances by ships gauge and record readings.

6.17.2. Main Engine - Cylinder Liner Withdrawal

According to engine running hours record & class inspection plan, the yard must carry out the following:

- Withdraw liner, clean, and paint cooling surface.
- Replace with new rings (owners supply) and carry out pressure test.

Extra Jobs:

1. Removal of jacket.
2. Transportation to work shop.
3. Lapping and machining of landing surface.

6.17.3. Main Engine – Start Air Valves and Safety Valve

According to class inspection plan, the yard must carry out the following:
- Disconnect valve.
- Open up.
- Clean.
- Grind in.
- Inspection and adjustment on completion.

6.17.4. Main Engine – Fuel Oil Injection Valve

- Disconnect valve.
- Open up.
- Clean and grind in contact surface; carry out pressure test.

6.17.5. Main Engine Stuffing Box

According to engine running hours record & class inspection plan, the yard must carry out the following:

- Remove stuffing box to workshop.

- Open up, skim, and face up contact surfaces.
- Adjust gap or renew rings (owners supply).

6.17.6. Main Engine Bearing Inspection

According to engine running hours record & class inspection plan, the yard must carry out the following:

- Open up upper half.
- Clean, inspect, and check.
- Record clearances.
- Close up on completion.

6.17.7. Cross Head and Bottom End Bearing Inspection

According to engine running hours record & class inspection plan, the yard must carry out the following:

- Open up bearing for inspection of lower and upper halves.
- Clean, check, and record clearances.
- Close up on completion.

6.17.8. Main Thrust Bearing

According to engine running hours record & class inspection plan, the yard must carry out the following:
- Open up upper half, draw out pads, clean and inspect.
- Measure thrust and journal bearing clearances with feller gauge.
- Close up on completion.

164

6.17.9. Crankcase Cleaning

According to class inspection plan, the yard must carry out the following:

- Open up crankcase doors.
- Superintendent inspection.
- Clean crankcase and close up on completion.

6.17.10. Main Engine Crank Shaft Deflection

- Measure and record engine deflection afloat condition before entering dry dock and after un-docking.

6.17.11. Turbo Chargers Overhauling

According to engine running hours record & class inspection plan, the yard must carry out the following:

- Open up turbo chargers and clean all parts thoroughly.
- Measure and record clearances of the bearing and rotor shaft.
- Replace worn out parts (owners supply).
- Rotor balancing test.
- Reassemble and refit in good order.

6.17.12. Air Coolers

The yard must carry out the following:

- Disconnect and remove cooler.
- Clean sea water and air side with chemicals.
- Paint covers and water box.
- Renew zinc anodes (owners supply).
- Hydro test.
- Reassemble.

6.17.13. Heat Exchangers

The yard must carry out the following:

- Open up covers.
- Clean sea water side, water box, and cover interiors.
- Paint with one coat and renew zinc anodes (owners supply).
- Chemical cleaning.
- Hydro test.

6.17.14. Main Condenser

The yard must carry out the following:

- Open up manhole covers on both ends.
- Clean water box and tube plates.
- Blow clear tubes and renew zinc anodes (owners supply).
- Chemical cleaning.
- Hydro test.

6.17.15. Fire Tube Boiler Cleaning

According to class inspection plan, the yard must carry out the following:

- Remove access doors.
- Clean fire and water sides with fresh water.
- Survey and close after inspection.

The following are excluded:

- Hard scrapping or chipping of heavy deposits.
- Cleaning of air heaters.
- Opening of hand hole doors.
- Chemical cleaning.
- Hydro testing.
- Any repairs and renewals.
- Gaskets (owners supply).

6.17.16. Water Tube Boiler Cleaning

According to class inspection plan, the yard must carry out the following:

- Open access doors for cleaning and wash down fire sides with fresh water.
- Open steam water drum doors, head clean drums, and close after inspection.

The following are excluded:

- Hard scrapping or chipping of heavy deposits.
- Cleaning of air heaters.
- Opening of hand hole doors.
- Chemical cleaning.
- Hydro testing.
- Any repairs and renewals.
- Gaskets (owners supply).

6.17.17. Main Steam Turbine

According to the operation manual instruction class inspection plan, the yard must carry out the following:

- Disconnect steam pipe and insulation.
- Install ships lifting tool.
- Open and lift upper casing for examination/survey.
- Measure labyrinth clearance and close on completion.

The following are excluded:

- Insulation.
- Adjusting the labyrinth.
- Repair and renewals.
- Opening of control gear.

6.17.18. Main Steam Turbine Bearing

According to the operation manual instruction class inspection plan, the yard must carry out the following:

- Open up, clean, and examine forward and aft journal and thrust bearing.
- Measure, clearance, and close on completion.

6.17.19. Main Steam Turbine Flexible Coupling

According to the operation manual instruction class inspection plan, the yard must carry out the following:

- Open up coupling for cleaning and examination.
- Survey, measure, and record clearances.
- Close on completion.

The following are excluded:

- Checking and adjustment alignment.
- Repair and renewals.

6.17.20. Alternator Turbine - Turbine Side

According to the operation manual instruction class inspection plan, the yard must carry out the following:

- Disconnect steam pipes for access.
- Open up casing, rotor bearing, and coupling.
- Lift up rotor using ships lifting tool.
- Check labyrinth.
- Measure bearing clearances.
- Check rotor with dial gauge.
- Close on completion.

6.17.21. Alternator Turbine - Reduction Gear

According to the operation manual instruction class inspection plan, the yard must carry out the following:

- Open up casing pinion, and gear bearing top halves.
- Clean and check back lash of gears.
- Measure clearances and close on completion.

6.17.22. Compressors Overhauling

The yard must carry out the following:

- Open up cylinders covers and crank pin bearing.
- Draw pistons.
- Renew ring, if necessary (owners supply).
- Remove piston pins.
- Open up main bearings.
- Clean and face up suction and delivery valves for inspection.
- Cleaning of air cooler to be included.

6.17.23. Air Bottles

The yard must carry out the following:

- Open up manholes.
- Clean and wipe dry interior for inspection.
- On completion, paint owners supply air bottle.
- Refit manholes with new gaskets.

6.17.24. Ship System Valves Overhauling

According to listed valves by C/E, the yard must carry out the following:

- Opening up listed globe and gate valve for in situ overhaul.
- Disconnecting and removing cover, spindle and gland, cleaning all exposed parts, hand grinding of globe valve, light hand scraping of gate valve.
- Testing bedding in presence of ship's superintendent.
- Paint internal exposed areas and reassembling with new cover joint and repacking gland.

6.17.25. Oil tanker Cargo Pumps Overhauling

According to the operation manual instruction class inspection plan, the yard must carry out the following:

- Disconnecting and removing top half of casing.
- Releasing shaft flexible coupling from drive.
- Slinging and removing impeller, shaft and wearing rings.
- Withdraw impeller, shaft sleeve, and bearings from shaft.
- Cleaning all exposed parts, calibrating, and reporting.
- Reassembling as before using owner's supplied parts.
- Operation test in presence of ship's superintendent.

6.17.26. Ship System Pumps (centrifugal-type)

Overhauling

As per ship technical superintendent instruction, the yard must carry out the following:

- Disconnecting and removing top half of casing.
- Release shaft coupling from motor drive.
- Slinging and removing impeller, shaft, and wearing rings.
- Withdraw impeller, shaft sleeve, and bearings from shaft.
- Cleaning all exposed parts, calibrating and reporting.
- Reassembly as before using owners supplied parts.
- Operation test in presence of ship's superintendent.

6.17.27. Ship System Pumps (reciprocating-type pumps, steam driven) Overhauling

As per ship technical superintendent instruction, the yard must carry out the following:

- Disconnecting and removing steam cylinder top cover.
- Release steam piston, withdrawing, removing piston rings.
- Clean, calibrate, and recording.
- Disconnecting and removing slide valve cover.
- Removing valves, cleaning, and presenting for survey.
- Disconnecting and removing bucket cover.
- Release bucket, withdrawing, removing bucket rings.
- Clean, calibrate, and recording.
- Opening up suction and delivery valve chest.

- Remove the valves and springs.
- Cleaning, grinding, and presenting for survey.
- Fully reassemble complete pump, renewing all jointing and repacking glands with owner's supplied.
- Operation test in presence of ship's superintendent.

6.17.28. Ship System Pumps (reciprocating-type pumps, electric motor driven) Overhauling

As per ship technical superintendent instruction, the yard must carry out the following:

- Disconnecting, removing electric motor, and putting it aside.
- Disconnecting and removing bucket cover.
- Releasing bucket, with-drawing, removing bucket rings.
- Cleaning, calibrating, and recording.
- Opening up suction and delivery valve chest.
- Removing valves and springs, cleaning, grinding, and presenting for survey.
- Fully reassemble complete pump, renewing all jointing and repacking glands with owner's supplied.
- Reinstalling electric motor and making terminals.
- Operation test in presence of ship's superintendent.

6.17.29. Steering Pump Overhauling

As per ship technical superintendent instruction, the yard must carry out the following:
- Disconnecting pump and removing for in situ overhaul.

- Open up pump, full dismantling, cleaning calibrating and presenting for survey.
- Fully reassemble using owner's supplied spares and reinstalling in place.

6.17.30. Gear Pump Overhauling

As per ship technical superintendent instruction, the yard must carry out the following:

- Disconnecting and removing pump, opening up end covers, withdrawing gear units, cleaning, calibrating, recording clearances, and presenting them for survey.
- Fully reassemble pump, renewing all jointing and repacking glands with owner's supplied packing or seals.

6.18. Electrical Works

6.18.1. Switchboard Cleaning

As per ship technical superintendent instruction &the item for class inspection, the yard must carry out the following:

- Cleaning behind switchboard.
- Examining all connections and retightening as necessary.
- Reporting conditions.

6.18.2. Electrical Motors Overhauling

As per ship technical superintendent instruction & according to motor repair list, the yard must carry out the following:

- Disconnecting motor from location.
- Transporting motor ashore to workshop for rewinding.
- Receiving motor in workshop, dismantling, cutting out all stator coils, removing rotor bearings, and cleaning all parts.
- Forming new stator coils in copper wire assembling, using new insulation and varnish.
- Baking dry in oven, dip varnishing and re-baking in oven. Reassembling all parts, fitting new standard type ball or roller bearings to rotor and testing in workshop.
- Returning motor back on board and refitting in original position and reconnecting original cables.
- Final operation test on-board in presence of ship's superintendent.

6.18.3. Electric Generators (alternators) Overhauling

According to ship technical superintendent instruction & class plan for inspection, the yard must carry out the following:

- Disconnecting and removing rotor ashore to workshop.
- Full cleaning, baking in oven, drying, varnishing, and re-baking in oven.
- Workshop testing in presence of ship's superintendent.
- Return it back on-board.

- Reassembling and reconnecting in place on board.
- Alignment to be carried out and reported.
- Operation test on-board in presence of ship's superintendent.

Chapter 7: The Ship Repair Yard Operation Departments

The Technical Superintendent is attending the dry dock for managing the repair activities on-board the ship.

And he will be in direct contact with the yard production departments and ship repair management department.

In this chapter, I will identify the shipyard production department's duties and responsibilities which may be different from one shipyard to another.

"For further information about the shipyard whole organization, it is available in my book: Ship Repair Project Managers Guide/ Chapter 2"

7.1. HSSE Department

The Technical Superintendent and the shipyard SRM are responsible to ensure that safety precautions, security level, health & environment conditions during the ship stay in the shipyard for repair.

The Technical Superintendent to ensure that the Safety induction has been given to his ship crew upon ship arrives to the yard; this section has been produced in order to introduce the shipyard HSSE responsibilities.

Main Roles & Responsibilities

The HSSE Department seeks to provide necessary HSSE information, HSSE planning and strategy for HSSE efficiency; it minimizes incidents and accidents by strengthening HSSE policy and control and establishes proper process and procedure for enhancing efficiency.

Health & Safety Section

- To develop and implement health and safety procedures.
- Safety control on-board and for yard facilities/managing safety equipment.
- Health and safety control on-board and for yard facilities including gas free tests.
- To provide HSSE trainings as per HSSE training manual.
- To implement and maintain ISO 9001:2008 and OHSAS 18001:2007.
- Managing occupational health in all yard facilities such dormitory and management housing.
- To provide Health & Safety trainings as per HSSE training manual.

Firefighting & Rescue Section

- Managing and operating clinic/rescue/firefighting equipment,
- To prepare company environment policy.

- Fire prevention, extinguishing, and emergency response.
- Coordination with civil Defense.

Security Section

- Managing the security policy of company.
- To carry out security tasks for protecting the yard and other assets outside of the shipyard.
- Operating guard security team.
- To issue and control passes for visitors/guest/ship-owners, meeting the security standards and requirements of IPA, ISPS codes and SOLAS.
- To co-ordinate with govt. authorities for security issues such coast guard and navy.

Environment Section

- To develop and implement environmental policies and procedures.
- To establish and maintain the environmental management system to be in line with ISO 14001/2004.
- To co-ordinate with govt. authorities for environmental issues and necessary licenses.
- To coordinate and oversee the compliance of environmental requirements.

7.2. QA/QC Department

The Technical Superintendent and the shipyard SRM is responsible to ensure the quality standards of the repair activities on-board the ship and this section has been produced in order to introduce the ship yard QA/QC responsibilities.

Main Roles & Responsibilities

To provide necessary quality information related with quality planning & control, to conduct education of efficient and appropriate quality control, to supervise the technical aspects, the inspection progress and quality of projects.

Quality Assurance Section

- Quality plan and company standard control.
- ISO 9000, 14000 series certifying and managing.
- To provide technical support and development in quality control.
- NDT services and control.
- To prepare different quality certificates as per business needs.

Quality Control Section

- Quality control for repair and new construction work such as steel structure, machinery, outfitting, piping, and electric work.

- Inspection, testing, and measurement report control coordinate with the ship's surveyor and representative for inspection, testing, and surveying.
- To manage re-inspection ratio of each production department.

7.3. Contract & Procurement Department

The Technical Superintendent and the shipyard SRM are responsible for tracking well the materials & service providers that are required for his project repair activities.

This section has been produced in order to introduce the shipyard C&P Department responsibilities.

Main Role & Responsibility

The C&P Department focuses on timely purchase of goods and services, reduces the lead time, gets involved in early discussion of projects, and establishes related policy and procedures.

Contract & Procurement Section

- To set standard terms and conditions for contracts and agreements (approved by the legal department).

- To issue a contract for services and outsourcing ad set-up, mobilizing lead time.

- To find, evaluate, and register a reliable supplier in the vendor list (20% supplies should be local).

- To establish long/short term contracts for service and manpower sub-contractors in co-ordination with production.

- To submit contract, invoice, and other supporting documents to finance so as to process payments on time.

- To prepare material budget, set proper cost saving measures in each purchase of goods and services, and budget control to achieve annual cost saving targets.

- To handle the secretariat of tender committee and to provide all related supporting documents.

Logistics Section

- Transportation of materials from supplier to shipyard and customs clearance of materials (i.e. road, sea, and air freight).

- To manage taxes and invoices of materials including inspection of materials.

- Coordinate with government entities for obtaining of licenses such as import/export permits, custom duty, environmental permits, etc.

7.4. Marketing Department

Prior to ship arrival to the shipyard & during the repair specification preparation, The Technical Superintendent will start to communicate with the shipyard marketing department for requesting yard quotation, prices negotiation and dry dock firm booking.

This section has been produced in order to introduce the marketing processes & responsibilities.

Main Roles & Responsibilities

The Marketing Department carries out sales activity, promoting, estimation of projects, and preparation of quotation, invoicing, project management for the purpose of maximizing yard business.

Planning Section

- To set marketing strategy and conduct market analysis/issuing marketing reports.
- Preparation of business expansion such as offshore repair.
- To manage external advertisement/website.

Marketing Section (Area Wise)

- The promotion of the yard, market development, enlargement, and strengthening.
- Contacting clients and maintaining a relationship with them.
- Determining client qualifications and credibility.
- Setting up the company's marketing policy in terms of price, discounts, credit period, quality, delivery, etc.
- Preparing and submitting offers to clients.
- Preparing offers for damaged vessels/issuing order confirmations and concluding contracts.
- Preparing pre-qualification documents.
- Settling payments and bank guarantees.
- Performing advertising, branding activities and documentary films related to company business.
- To communicate with media for press releases, supplements, interviews, etc. ...and manage the company's corporate gifts.
- Controlling regional and international agents and preparing long term contract with them.

Estimation Section

- The reception and review of docking indents and repair/conversion specifications from clients.
- The collection of all information and data from relevant departments to prepare quotation/offer.
- Analysis of repair/conversion specification.

- Preparing quotation including work volume, quantity, time duration, and price.
- Setting the unit price of each detailed work order (tariffs) with coordination of production and concerned department.
- Analyzing the cost structure such as labor, materials, and overhead cost.
- Updating tariffs, quotations, bills, and other documents in coordination with production (same standard man-hour with estimation and production).
- To share project details with relevant department to plan for ship-repair/conversion.

7.5. Hull or Steel Department

The shipyard profit achieved mainly from the steel repairs and this lead to keep steel department on the top of the production divisions.

The Technical Superintendent is responsible for providing the yard with clear repair specification along with UTM drawings of the damage area.

Also, he is responsible for monitoring the repair quantities, qualities and delivery schedule.

This section has been produced in order to introduce the steel department responsibilities.

Main Roles & Responsibilities

- Hull processing shop operating (steel processing).
- Raw steel material control (arranging, cutting, and distribution).
- Minimize wastage of raw material.
- Steel marking on curves and various shapes.
- Conversion vessel marking control.
- Hull steel structure repair.
- New steel structure processing (block fabrication/erection).

7.6. Blasting & Painting Department

The blasting and painting also is very important to the ship yard and it is the second department in the production organization, also it is profit achieves to the ship yard.

The Technical Superintendent is responsible for clearing the area agreement with the shipyard, arranging the paint inspector, supply the paint on time, monitoring the treatment step by step and confirm the application quality with the paint inspector.

This section has been produced in order to introduce the blasting & painting department responsibilities.

Main Roles & Responsibilities

- Grit blasting or power tooling on steel structure.
- Outfitting/piping before painting.

- Painting by spray on hull steel structure or outfitting/piping.
- Touch-up carrying on paint damage parts.
- High pressure washing by water for removal of dust, rust, and salt.
- Arranging control of various paint equipment.
- Grit supplying to blasting machine.
- Ship's general cleaning/dock cleaning.
- Tank cleaning for hot work (hull, outfitting, piping, etc.).
- Tank/hold cleaning for painting (before/after).

7.7. Mechanical Department

The repairs of ship machineries & equipment is carried out according to the running hour's maintenance plan or inspection plan of the classification society and at operation problem case or operation failure.

The Technical Superintendent is responsible for providing the repair scope to the shipyard along with the technical data such as maker, serial numbers, equipment manual and drawings.

Also, he is responsible for repairing inspection in yard workshop, operation test on-board.

This section has been produced in order to introduce the mechanical department responsibilities.

Main Roles & Responsibilities

- M/Engine and aux. engine system overhaul, repair, and measurement.
- Aux. machinery system and cargo pump repair, and sea trial.
- Main or aux. boiler overhaul, cleaning, and repair.
- Various heat-exchanger repairs in E/R.
- Various engine parts machining in workshop.
- Boring for rudder, stern tube, and others engine parts.
- Welding, boring repair work for propulsion system.
- Steering gear and rudder system overhaul and repair/propulsion system overhaul and repair.
- Deck machinery repair/hydraulic system repair of various deck machinery.

7.8. Electrical Department

The repairs of ship electrical equipment, automation system, instrumentation items & navigation equipment is carried out according to the maker's maintenance plan or inspection plan of classification society and at operation problem case or operation failure.

The Technical Superintendent is responsible for providing the motors list to the shipyard; the list should include the motor location, KW, HZ, bearings serial numbers and any drawings related to the work.

Also, he is responsible for repairing inspection in yard workshop, operation test on-board.

This section has been produced in order to introduce the electrical department responsibilities.

Main Roles & Responsibilities

- Various motor and generator overhaul and repair.
- Electric panel such as M.S.B., local panel, start panel, etc.
- Power cable, lighting, switch, battery work, and sea trial.
- Radio, navigation, communication equipment repair, and calibration.
- Instrument equipment and maneuvering system calibration and repair.

7.9. Piping Department

The pipe work is carried out for damaged pipes on the ship pipeline systems or for adding a completely new pipeline system to the existing one or to modify some of pipeline.

The Technical Superintendent is responsible for providing the pipe list to the shipyard; the list should include the pipe location, pipe materials, size, flanges dimension and pipeline drawings if possible.

This section has been produced in order to introduce the piping department responsibilities.

Main Roles & Responsibilities

- Ship's pipe repair (in engine room, ballast tank, cargo tank, deck, accommodation, etc.).
- New and conversion of ship's pipe processing.
- Insulation work on E/R and deck piping.

7.10. Production Control or Production Planning

Unit Department

The production control department is for monitoring the performance of yard production team & control the repair work of the sub-contractor on-board the ship.

This section has been produced in order to introduce the production control department responsibilities.

Main Roles & Responsibilities

- To publish ship repair program with docking-undocking plan.
- Load curve control for production.
- Direct and In-direct man-hour (M/H) control (Plan & Result).
- Establish measure of productivity of manpower.
- Sub-contractor control of work completion.
- Ships repair/conversion progress control.
- Provide reports of delivered/on-progress projects.

7.11. Production Support or Yard Operation Department

This department is to support the yard in it is operation & provide the ship with all general services are required.

This section has been produced in order to introduce the production control department responsibilities.

Main Roles & Responsibilities

The main responsibility of the Production Support/Yard Operation Department is to ensure that the desired facilities are available at an optimum cost within safety guidelines. Additionally, it supports on time all necessary things for the production side such as all facilities, utilities, heavy transportation, production equipment, and tools.

Facility Management Section

- To control assets and do periodically preventive maintenance of facilities (super structure, buildings, etc.).
- To set preventive maintenance philosophy and manuals for all super structures and facilities.
- To develop cost saving and cost control methods; set up standards for consumption and compare them with the budget.
- Operation for plants (environmental facilities, gas plants, Air compressors, Substations).
- Operation for dock pumps and dock gates.

- Supply all utility (power, water, gas, etc.) supporting temporary utility, electric, and piping to work locations.
- Maintenance of all facilities, buildings, and civil contractures.
- Implementing different maintenance system and work orders - routine, planned, preventive, and breakdown maintenance.

Rigging & Lifting Section

- Operation for Heavy lift & Transportation equipment, jib cranes, and tower cranes.

Scaffolding Section

- Installation and dismantlement of scaffolding for all kinds of repair work.
- To manage and maintain scaffolding materials.

Dock Master Section

- Movement of ships for production.
- Arrangement of ships to dock and quay.
- Dock keel block arrangement and dock item work.

7.12. Ship Repair Management Department

Duties & Responsibilities

- Compilation of all information available from commercial file in order to prepare all standard documents necessary for the work and distribution to yard services concerned.

- Clarifications with customer representative of any unclear item in the customer specification resulting from detailed discussions with yard services.
- Board the vessel on way for inspection and reporting on arrival.
- Clarification and agreement with customer representative of required condition for the vessel on arrival as well as requirements for docking, taking into consideration specifications and yard procedures.
- Enquiry for availability of any technical information necessary for the works (drawing, specification, owner's decision on spare parts, etc.).
- Discussion and agreement with yard's services of the work preliminary schedule.
- Meeting with customer representative and staff on arrival, introducing them to the yard's normal practice safety regulations and procedures,
- Identification on site of specified works with the services concerned and agreement on technical aspects according to the yard's practice and capabilities.
- Follow-up works in progress and schedule of repairs, identifying deviations, processing eventual corrective measures to minimize idle time, maintain delivery dates, and optimizing the use of yard facilities/equipment.
- Attendance of meetings with customer representative and staff for discussion of all pertinent aspects of work, in particular, process variations of work and their effects on the schedule.

- Safety aspects and interference between the yard and customers staff work requirements for customer supplied items.
- Eventual receipt of complaints addressing the same to concerned yard services and, if required, process the same as per yard quality assurance system.
- Preparation of change orders and assistance on provision of details to sales department to allow preparation of quotations.
- Assurance that quality of work is commercially acceptable according to established procedures and obtain approval for work completed from customer representative.
- Attendance of production meetings to report on progress of work and relevant problems related with project.
- Maintenance of close and daily contacts with the yard's safety officers and the yard's services; initiate meeting, when required, with them and customer staff to agree on procedures, sequence, priorities of conflicting tasks, unsafe conditions, and measures to be taken to minimize any negative effect on the schedule.

Chapter 8: The Ship Repair Project Management Processes

This chapter has been produced in order to introduce in detail the repair project management to the technical superintendent from his request for shipyard quotation stage to ship delivery stage.

The technical superintendent must know the project management processes from repair specification preparation to ship delivery after work compilation.

8.1. Pre-Arrival Processes

Communication with the Shipyards:

- The technical superintendent is responsible for preparing the repair specification as mentioned earlier in chapter 6.
- Sending the repair specifications and docking intentions to the shipyards and request for the for-quotation purpose.
- Ship yard will review the repair specification to ensure that it has the full required information for estimation calculation such as ship particulars, ship drawings, steel dimensions or quantity, pipe length and

diameters, tanks size and volume, blasting and painting area, engines details, propellers dimensions, etc. any others technical data and drawings which can help estimation department in the estimation process; otherwise the yard should return back directly to the technical superintendent in order to clear with him all unclear items in his repair specification.

- Once the repair specification is completed it will be forwarded to the estimation department for estimation process.

Quotation Process:

- Estimation Department receives the full repair specification from the yard marketing team for preparing the quotations according to yard tariffs while analyzing the cost structure of the projects such as labors, materials, subcontractors or service engineer's arrangement and overhead cost.

- Estimators prepare the quotation of the repair specification activities, arrange, and list the quotation items with attaching shipyard main facilities information's such as:

1. Repair berths numbers, drafts, and lengths.
2. Dry dock numbers, dead weight capacities, minimum depth of water, length and width.

3. Floating dock numbers, dock lifting capacity, length, width, dock cranes and crane lifting capacity.
4. Yard cranes numbers, cranes location, lifting capacity for each and maximum outreach for each.
5. Floating cranes numbers and the lifting capacity for each.
6. Tugboat numbers and bollard pull capacity for each.

Quotation general remarks such as:

1. All prices quote is in USD and are subject to variation due to changes in cost and availability of material.
2. All prices quoted for repairs carried out in our yard premises.
3. All prices are based on work being carried out during normal working hours.
4. All prices are quoted unless mentioned in the tariff excluding removals for access, staging, cleaning, rust freeing, testing, painting, ventilation, and lighting.
5. All work to be carried out as per yard general terms, conditions, and yard safety regulations.
6. Yard working hours and official holidays.

- After the yard estimators have completed the price list of the repair specification, the yard marketing in-charge will review it once more, and then he should return it back to the estimators for any miscalculation, missing items or unclear items until setting up the full correct price list.

- Next, sending the yard tender to the technical superintendent consists of the quotation covering (price list), yard terms and conditions, dry dock firm booking, repair schedule, and ship delivery.

- Here, the negotiation exchanges will start between ship technical superintendent and the yard marketing around the price wise, docking period, delivery date and/or various items on yard terms and conditions.

- After the yard marketing in-charge person has fixed all the negotiated points with ship owners according to yard top management instructions, he must prepare the final tender agreement for approvals from yard managers and ship owner - owner will revert back to the yard with his confirmation for firm booking and tender.

- The shipyard marketing in-charge person will reply to the ship technical superintendent with yard acceptance firm booking then issuing the orders confirmation with identification code.

Preparing the Project for dry docking

It is very important that the technical superintendent to prepare the project at an earlier stage as soon as possible, such as:

- Prepare integrates hard copies of the project including information, specification, quotation, term and condition, correspondences, owner firm booking confirmation, yard firm booking acceptance, etc.
- Prepare for spare parts supply by issuing the purchase orders and follow up with the suppliers the delivery status on time and before ship arrive to the shipyard.
- Prepare for paints supply by issuing the purchase orders and follow up with the suppliers the delivery status on time and before ship arrive to the shipyard.
- Coordinate with the paint inspector and confirm the estimated date of attendance.
- Coordinate with the class surveyor and confirm with him the visiting schedule during the dry dock repair.
- Coordinate with the service engineers for their attendance and the repair schedule.
- Try to carry out the steel thickness measurements during the ship loading and un-loading at each port in order to minimize the dry-docking time.
- Confirm with the ship crew that all manuals of the ship equipment are available on-board and in good condition.

- Confirm with the ship crew that all the ship drawings are available on-board and in good condition.
- According to the above mentioned, the technical superintendent is responsible to initiate the initial repair plan.

8.2. After Ship Arrive to the dry docking

Shipyard Kick Off & Safety Meeting:

- This meeting should take place on the first working day after ship arrival at the yard. The ship repair manager should start the meeting by introducing himself as the yard in-charge person for the repairs. Additionally, he should give his telephone number to the technical superintendent, for easy contact during office hours or overnight in case of emergency.

- The ship repair manager should then introduce yard in-charge personnel attending the meeting starting with the yard safety officer.

- The yard safety officer would then give a short description for yard safety rules and highlight the on-board safety procedures in particular.

- The technical superintendent must mention clearly that all orders have to be channeled through him only to avoid misunderstanding and to ensure that the order has been passed to the right department in the yard.

- The technical superintendent has to agree with the yard SRM on a suitable time for daily on-board meetings.

Works Identification

The technical superintendent is responsible for Identification on site all works with the shipyard SRM and the concerned department to agree on the technical aspects according to the yards practice and capabilities.

Daily Meeting On-Board

During this meeting, the ship repair manager briefs the technical superintendent and ship crew on the progress of repair highlighting the difficulties, if any, due to shortage of spares, lateness of decision, or unclear identification of various items.

All change orders should be discussed with the technical superintendent during this meeting before issuing them to production departments.

Ship Dock in Follow-Up:

The technical superintendent is responsible for the following:

- Request from the ship master the ship ballast condition with zero list.
- Send the ballast conditions to the yard SRM for approval.
- Check with the yard dock master the keel block arrangement progress.
- Confirm with the ship master the yard docking plan (date and time).
- Confirm with the ship master the ship machinery conditions such as mooring winches, generators, ship cranes, ballast pump, etc.
- Follow up with pilot the entering progress.
- Confirm with the ship master that the ship has received all required services inside the dock such as electrical shore connection, cooling connection, gangway, etc.

Work Follow-Up During Repair Period

The technical superintendent is responsible for the following:

- Follow-up the work progress and the repair schedule
- identifying any deviations while processing eventual corrective measures to minimize idle time
- Maintain delivery dates and optimize the use of yard facilities/equipment

Focusing on the Critical Items such as:

The technical superintendent is responsible for the following:

- Steel work progress, especially inside the tanks.
- Blasting and painting progress, especially tank treatment.
- Spare parts supply or service arrangement by owner to be followed up at every meeting with the head office at every meeting or phone calls.
- Spare parts supply or service arrangement by yard to be followed up with yard procurement at every moment through the yard SRM.
- Tested items such as load test, MPI, etc. should be considered priority and expect test failure to affect the project's progress.
- Class item can affect repair progress because of class surveyor's notifications and remarks.
- Items on-hold by the owner office is to be followed up with the head office at every meeting or phone calls.
- Additional works to be started immediately unless there are no spares or materials are needed for supply.
- Ship undocking follow-up procedure.
- Receive ballast condition from ship's master for the yard approval.
- Ensure that the ship has received all the ballast water quantities required for undocking the ship safely.

Check that all Under Water Items (undocking items) Have been done (not limited to the below mentioned):

The technical superintendent is responsible for the following:

- Sea valves and filters are tightened in place.
- Bottom plugs are tightened in place and tested with vacuum tester.
- Hull-painting, touch up, and marking has been completed.
- Steel repair under water has been completed, tested, and approved by class.
- Sea chest has been closed after the technical superintendent inspection and approval.
- Ballast valves are tightened in place.
- Lift up anchor and chains.
- Rudder and propellers are in place.
- Echo sounder and speed log has been tested with vacuum tester.
- Any other items that can be effect on ship undocking.

Un-Docking Follow-Up Procedure:

The technical superintendent is responsible for the following:

- With the yard SRM, ensure that all in-charge engineers and their workers required for ship undocking are available on-board during the start of filling water in the dock.

- With the ship master, ensure that the ship crew in their position.

- Agree with yard SRM that to stop filling water in-side the dock before the ship becomes afloat in order to check with the yard engineers if any water leakage inside the engine room, pump room, etc.

- In case there is water leakage, the technical superintendent must directly contact to the yard SRM informing him; never start continuous filling of water till receiving ship master final confirmation.

- Once the ship becomes afloat with no leakage, the technical superintendent has to ask the chief engineer to start up the ship's generator.

- After ship generator is running, the technical superintendent has to give the order to the shipyard to disconnect shore power.

Sea Trial Follow-Up Procedure:

The technical superintendent is responsible for the following:

- The Sea trial will be carried out by ship crew and shipyard staff in order to check the condition of main engine and anything attached to it (governor, turbocharger, etc.).

- The technical superintendent will attend to the sea trial for coordinating between the ship crew and yard staff.

- And make sure that the ship is ready for delivery without any problems.

Work Completion Reports Follow-Up

The technical superintendent is responsible for reviewing the work completion report, and to confirm that it is prepared as per the actual repairs have been done on-board the ship.

Final Bills Negotiation

The technical superintendent is responsible for attending the final bill negotiation with the yard ship repair estimator in order to confirm together that all items have been carried out by the ship yard are covered in the final bill, without any doubt between the ship technical superintendent and the ship yard estimator.

Chapter 9: The Ship Crew Duties during the Dry Dock

The technical superintendent is responsible for ship repair and ship operation. And he needs to ensure the good performance of ship crew for managing the dry dock activities.

This chapter produced to explain the ship crew duties on-board the ship during the dry dock period.

9.1. General

- The technical superintendent is responsible for ensuring that each vessel is dry-docked in accordance with Classification Society's rules.

- Special circumstances may occur that require the scheduled docking to be brought forward or deferred.

- In this case, the technical superintendent advises the vessel's owner and makes the necessary arrangements.

- Major refits may be required as a result of unforeseen damage, changes to International rules and regulations, or major modifications required by the vessel's owner.

- The advice of defect system of reporting is maintained. Each vessel's master/chief engineer reports, as necessary, any defects or repairs for inclusion in the docking specification.

- The technical superintendent prepares a full docking specification against information obtained from:

  - Classification Society requirements
  - Owners requirements
  - Inspection reports
  - Planned maintenance reports
  - Advice of defects report
  - Incident/damage reports
  - Masters/Chief Engineers reports
  - Changes in legislation, national, port state, and International.

- The docking/refit specification contains advice on the vessel's date of availability and defines the work to be covered in the following areas:

  - General services
  - Dry-docking
  - Hull preparation
  - Painting
  - Steel repairs/renewals
  - Deck repairs
  - Engine repairs
  - Electrical repairs

- o Accommodation repairs
- o Outside contractors
- o Surveys

- The completed specification is checked for accuracy and detail and then presented to the technical manager for authorization.

9.2. Inspection and Verification

- All dry-docking/major refits are attended by at least the technical superintendent.

- In conjunction with the technical superintendent, the vessel's senior officers monitor the work carried out on board for compliance with the repair specification.

- All maintenance work carried out by ships staff or sub-contractors is recorded in the VFS on board and by the company.

9.3. Reporting

- The attending S/E forwards progress/status reports, in writing, to the technical superintendent.

- On completion of the docking, a full dry-dock repair report is prepared.

- This report is forwarded to the owner and copies kept in the VFS on board and by the company.

- A dry docking/repair analysis form is prepared and forwarded to the owner if required and kept in the VFS on board and by the company.

9.4. Alterations of Fittings

- No structural alterations to the vessel or her fittings, including the re-locating of safety equipment, shall be made without the sanction of the company.

- Should this sanction be obtained then the master and the chief engineer must ensure that the appropriate drawings on board are correctly amended.

- Copies of amended drawings must be forwarded to the company with all changes highlighted in order for the office copies of the same drawings to be similarly amended.

- Stability information must reflect any substantial changes BEFORE the vessel leaves the shipyard or repair berth.

- The master and the C/E must liaise with the company on this matter as a matter of extreme importance.

- Additional steelwork may result in the requirement for an inclining experiment to be carried out.

9.5. Supervision of Repairs

- It is usual for all work in connection with the dry-docking, repair, and upkeep of the ship to be carried out under the supervision of the vessel's S/E.

- Additions to the original specification shall not be put in hand without the permission of the technical superintendent.

- It is the responsibility of the vessel's staff to thoroughly test and prove satisfactory all repairs and for quality control and report any defects to the technical superintendent.

- Regular meetings between the vessel's senior officers, superintendent, and repairer are held to monitor work progress, discuss difficulties, and work schedule.

9.6. Dry Docking

- Before entry into dry-dock, the C/E is responsible for ensuring that the bilge wells and engine room tank tops are dry and that all double bottom tank lids are in place and secured.

- Fire pumps, sanitary pumps, and sewage unit pumps are to be isolated when the vessel is dry-docked, and the shore fire main has been connected.

- Before the vessel enters dry dock, the C/E and C/O must discuss and decide upon the distribution of both ballast and bunkers to obtain the correct docking condition and thus avoid undue stress to the hull when the vessel takes the blocks.

Records of the draft forward and aft, and the ullages or dips of water or oil in double bottom tanks, peaks, cofferdams and bunker compartments, must be entered in the E/R and deck logbooks.

9.7. Dry Dock Inspection

When the dock is dry, the outside and bottom of the hull, propeller, rudder etc. must be inspected by the master, chief Engineer and the technical superintendent to ascertain the condition and if any damage has been sustained since the previous docking.

9.8. Gas Free Certificate

- During repair periods no space is to be considered gas free unless a gas free certificate has been obtained and maintained.

- The certificate must state whether the space is gas free for hot work or entry only.

9.9. Boiler Blow Down

When it is necessary to steam a boiler during dry dockings, the blow down valves and cocks must be secured to prevent accidental discharge into the dry dock.

9.10. Undocking

- Prior to flooding the dock, the C/E and master will satisfy themselves that all drain plugs are properly fitted and that all sea valves are shut.

- All such plugs should be held by C/O while being removed.

- Distribution of weight and trim of the ship must be the same on leaving dry dock as on entering.

- Special sanction must be obtained from the S/E in charge of repairs and from the docking authorities for any departure from this instruction.

- The C/E is to station officers to inspect all sea connections and hull repairs while the dry dock is being flooded.

- Flooding is to be stopped before the vessel lifts off the blocks and a full examination is to be carried out to ensure that the vessel is watertight.

About the Author

Professional Projects Manager and Independent Marine Surveyor Consultancy of Ship Building | Ship Repair | Dry Docking | Ship Conversions | Ports and Shipping | Offshore Oil Rigs | Oil and Gas | Maritime Industry.

Eng. Mohamed Khamis
engkhames@yahoo.com

Bachelor's Degree of Marine and Naval Architecture Engineering
Egyptian | Birth Date: 20.02.1976 | Living in Oman.

He has vast, rich experiences worldwide in marketing of ship building, ship repair, dry docking, offshore, ship conversions, oil rigs and maritime industry with strong familiarization in the project management, yard production and operation management, tendering and estimation, technical resource optimization, manpower mobilization, cost control, international maritime organization requirements and rules application with focusing on QA/QC and HSE rules and regulations.

He has worked in different international reputable companies such as:

(ASRY) Arab Shipbuilding and Repair Yard	Bahrain
(ODC) Oman Drydock Company	Oman
(ASY) Alexandria Shipyard	Egypt
(ENC) Egyptian Navigation Company	Egypt
(ESRBC) Egyptian Ship Repair and Building	Egypt
(EAMS) Egyptian Authority for Maritime Safety	Egypt
Mahoney Shipping Company	Egypt
Al Shanfari Marine Services LLC	Oman

On Jun 2018 he has written his first book "Ship Repair Project Managers Guide", the book is visible at Amazon stores.

www.ingramcontent.com/pod-product-compliance
Lightning Source LLC
Chambersburg PA
CBHW031430270326
41930CB00007B/645